# THE BASKETBALL BOOK FOR BOYS 9-12

## THE HISTORY OF THE GAME, BIOGRAPHIES OF THE GREATEST PLAYERS OF ALL TIME, STORIES OF AMAZING GAMES, AND INCREDIBLE FACTS

### JIMMY MCCALL

TOMOKAI RIVER

# CONTENTS

# Get Your Kids into the Game

Want to know how to really get your kid
into basketball?

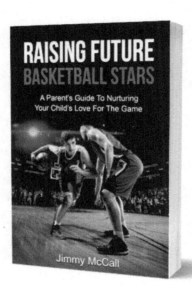

Get this short, free eBook delivered straight to your inbox,
by joining the Tomokai Launch Squad by scanning the QR
code below.

You'll also get access to all of our books ahead of
publication, absolutely free.

# INTRODUCTION

Growing up, my parents always knew where I was. It's not because I told them that I was going to my room, or to the back yard, or down the street. I didn't have to say anything.

They could just hear me playing sports.

Sometimes I'd be tossing a football with friends on the street. We'd lose our minds when someone caught a bomb of a touchdown pass by the stop sign, and did a celebratory dance that made us all crack up.

I would also play baseball in the area, as we tried to direct our scalding line drives away from windows and cars. Instead of using actual baseballs, we'd use tennis balls and aluminum bats to showcase some serious childhood power in the chalk-drawn batter's box.

Basketball also had a special place in my heart during my youth.

When I was in middle school, I remember going to the NBA store and buying a San Antonio Spurs hoop and mini basketball for my bedroom. It was one of those hoops you could attach to the very top of your door. Much to my parents' dismay, the walls were used as backboards for some of the smoothest bank shots and most powerful self-assisted alley-oop dunks in the history of bedroom basketball.

I would later graduate to playing with friends in the neighborhood at the park or in my back yard. While the prospect of grabbing on to the rim after a dunk was out of the question, seeing the basketball go through the hoop while hearing that distinctive "swish" sound made the game even more appealing.

But the truth was, I didn't really need any of these settings to grow my love for the sport. If I wasn't able to get to a hoop, I would get creative. Rolling up socks into a ball, and shooting it into the hamper would've been just as satisfying, especially as a youngster.

There were so many times when an NBA game would be on TV, and I'd look around for any type of clothing (dirty or not) to roll up so I could imitate one of the pros. Don't bother looking for any video footage of this, I promise there wasn't any!

You may be wondering: But wasn't there one moment he can remember that was the true beginning of his love for basketball?

I can't single out one particular magical moment, but maybe that's the point.

Basketball is a sport that highlights the teamwork needed to win a game, and the strategy necessary to come up with a plan to defeat an opponent.

It's a game that tests your physical ability, but also brings out personality traits that you didn't know you had. It teaches lessons of hard work and sacrifice through a sport that you don't need to buy expensive equipment to play.

It's a game that shows you that skill and talent can come from anyone, regardless of what they look like or where they come from.

Basketball is an experience that keeps on giving, and there's nothing in the world I'd trade that for.

# 1

# THE HISTORY OF BASKETBALL

After you've finished your chores and done your homework, tune into an NBA basketball game and take in everything that's going on. When I say *everything*, I mean it.

Focus on the players, the coaches and the referees. Look at the people sitting in courtside seats, at the bench, and the entire arena. Think about how everything has to come together perfectly in order for a two-and-a-half-hour game to take place, to create a product that's beloved by people all over the world.

Check your social media feed during halftime. There's an excellent chance that clips from the game you've been watching are already posted on Instagram or

Facebook, and even have hundreds, if not thousands, of comments or likes.

The game has evolved into something that anyone can engage with at home, on the go, or in person at the arena.

But it wasn't always like that.

Celebrities didn't always pay thousands of dollars to feel the breeze of professional players running past them as they sat courtside.

Game officials didn't always have the ability to check instant replay to see if there was a close call.

The games weren't even always broadcast on live TV, which is pretty crazy to think about, right?

Basketball was invented a very long time ago. Over the course of more than a hundred years, the sport has grown into what it is today.

Some of the brightest minds in science are working on ways to allow humans to time travel. But until they figure it out, step into this basketball time machine with me to understand how the sport began, and how it's changed over the years.

## HOW IT ALL BEGAN

I don't know where you're reading this book, but there's at least a chance you're in a part of the United States (or the world) that gets mighty chilly when winter arrives. Walking around your neighborhood when the temperature is below freezing and the wind is howling makes it seem like your ears are going to fall off. It's tempting to stay home, curl up in a cozy blanket, and watch TV with your friends and family during these days.

That can be super relaxing, but it can also be boring to do every day until the weather warms up in the spring. Plus, sitting around for several months without exercise isn't good for any kid (or adult, for that matter).

A long time ago, in 1891, a physical education teacher at the International YMCA Training School in Massachusetts, named James Naismith, was given two weeks to come up with a game that would be athletic, not take up too much room, help the track students stay in shape while indoors during the harsh winter months and that was fair for all players.

Naismith asked what materials were available to him, and the janitor brought him two peach baskets. This didn't seem like much help, but it provided the resourceful man some inspiration.

Naismith decided to nail the peach baskets to two balconies on either side of the school's gym. As it turned out, the bottom of the balconies were 10 feet high, which is the same height that regulation basketball hoops are today.

Naismith had no idea what would happen next. Would his rowdy students like the game? Did he have a good enough plan to keep the players safe?

There were only a couple of rules at first, which led the players to engage in all sorts of things that were legal in other sports, but are things we don't recognize in today's basketball games. The students were tackling each other, holding one another, not dribbling and were throwing the ball towards the peach basket rather than shooting it.

It was utter chaos.

Naismith also had to find a way to keep the game moving after someone made a shot. Like any regular basket used for a picnic, these peach baskets had bottoms. As a result, the ball would go into the basket, and just stay there.

To avoid delays, he recruited two men to be stationed on the balconies. They would retrieve the ball from the basket and throw it back down so the game could continue.

This picture isn't exactly the same one we're used to when we think about how basketball is played today. But for something that Naismith came up with so quickly, it was a huge success. His students really enjoyed this new sport, and wanted to keep playing it during the winter of 1891-1892.

But Naismith knew he had to come up with more rules to keep the game from being a free-for-all, and to make sure the players did not get hurt. He introduced the concept of fouls, which would penalize the defense if they committed too many infractions. If the ball went out of bounds, a player could pass the ball back in bounds, but would only have five seconds to do so. That rule is actually still valid today at all levels of basketball!

Of course, it occurred to all the participants that retrieving the ball from the basket was an unnecessary step, so it was later decided that the bottom of the basket would be cut off so a successful shot would go right through the goal.

## HOW THE GAME HAS CHANGED

It didn't take very long for word to spread about the sport. In fact, during that same decade, other universities throughout the United States adopted the game. James Naismith himself would go on to work at the University of Kansas, and would serve as the head coach of the Jayhawks, the men's basketball team, from 1898-1906. What's kind of funny is that the Jayhawks lost more games than they won during that timeframe, even though they were coached by the guy who invented the sport!

In the early part of the 1900's, basketball would take off all around the country. The fast-moving nature of the sport, coupled with the idea that specialized gear was not needed to participate, became appealing to the masses. Even though the final score of the games was pretty low, fans enjoyed the continuous action.

During the infancy of the sport, the most popular shot was the two-handed set shot. Players would run around the court looking for open space, and would use two hands to push the ball towards the rim, without jumping off the ground.

In the years that followed, certain players would take it to the next level by shooting towards the hoop with one leg already in the air. We might think of that shot today as a "runner," "floater" or traditional layup. This added to the excitement of the game because players realized they could score without necessarily standing still.

The sport had a solid foundation within the college ranks, but that's where it ended for the time being. After players graduated, there wasn't an obvious next step for them to continue playing professionally. Most players would transition to their adult lives and their regular jobs as firemen, plumbers, doctors, lawyers, and so on.

Even though large arenas like Madison Square Garden in New York would host college games, the sport needed to reach another tier of fame in order to keep growing. An important milestone was when basketball was included as an official sport in the 1936 Olympic Games. The United States would field a team of college players who would play against other young men from Poland, Mexico and Canada. There was only one problem.

The IOC (International Olympic Committee) didn't have a hardwood basketball floor available for games to be played on. It was decided that the competition would take place on a tennis court that was slightly adjusted for basketball. When we say slightly, we mean barely, if at all!

The "court," if you could call it that, was a dirt space with lines to indicate where the court began and ended. Because of the uncertain footing, players were nervous about running too quickly, or dribbling on an area that might be uneven.

The gold medal matchup between the United States and Canada presented one other wrinkle. It rained all day before the game was scheduled to be played, and all throughout the contest as well. The American and Canadian players had to essentially play basketball in the mud, while spectators watched from the stands holding umbrellas. The United States would capture the first basketball gold medal, defeating Canada 19-8 in a very soggy contest. Thankfully, Olympic basketball would never be played outdoors again.

Despite the somewhat questionable presentation of the sport on the world's stage in 1936, basketball was continuing its march into the hearts of American sports fans. Another landmark moment for the game took place in 1927, when a group of traveling showmen named the Harlem Globetrotters played their first game.

Founded by Abe Saperstein, the Globetrotters were created to showcase the fun and exciting side of basketball. The team didn't just want to win; they wanted to put on a show that made fans cheer, laugh and smile. When they first hit the court, they were an actual basketball team, focused on proving that they could beat some of the best collections of talent in the United States.

Thanks to their skills and flair for playing the game with style, the Globetrotters and their classic jingle became popular with fans. They would go on to defeat some future basketball Hall of Famers in the ensuing decades, and basketball Hall of Famers also decided to play with them. The Harlem Globetrotters helped players and fans alike realize what the sport could turn into with their fast break passes, long range shooting and slam dunk plays.

The Globetrotters are still around today, as you may know, and remain committed to making fans happy while running circles around their opponents in what is basically "basketball theater."

With all this positive momentum swirling, there was only one big thing left for the game of basketball to do: Start a successful professional league!

There had been some attempts during this time to play the game at the highest level for money. Regional leagues would pop up in Massachusetts and in cities like Philadelphia and New York, but their interest was limited to people who lived in those areas.

Two leagues were the most successful in the 1940's; the NBL (National Basketball League) and BAA (Basketball

Association of America). Both operations had established successful franchises in different parts of the United States and Canada, and in 1949 they decided to join forces to create the league that we know and love today; the NBA!

The NBA would be the go-to destination for big time talent coming out of college in the 1950's and 1960's. Thanks to relocation and business savvy owners, the league would expand to the West Coast and have a following throughout the United States. Things were really taking off, as fans became obsessed with their favorite teams and players.

The league would receive a stiff challenge from 1967-1976 from a new league called the ABA (American Basketball Association). The ABA marketed themselves as a more fun, futuristic league, which could entertain fans better than the NBA could. The ABA had a three-point line, and encouraged high scoring games without too much defense being played.

The ABA was also not afraid to pay their players a lot of money, which attracted some top talent to their league. The NBA was still the most popular league, but the ABA was quickly gaining fans.

As it turned out, the ABA was not able to sustain the business, but they had an important influence on the

NBA, and on how basketball would be played moving forward. After the ABA folded, the NBA absorbed four of its teams, and became a more enjoyable sport to watch.

There was another lesson the NBA learned from the ABA. The NBA had some great players, but it didn't always do its best to promote them in the media. Imagine a star player today not being on Twitter or Instagram!

That would all change in the 1980's, as the league welcomed Magic Johnson and Larry Bird. These two players and personalities immediately made the Los Angeles Lakers and Boston Celtics immensely popular, and the league began airing live games at night, when families could watch them together.

Michael Jordan would pick up where Bird and Johnson left off, and NBA commissioner David Stern focused on bringing fans closer to the game in the United States and across the world. In the 1990's, everyone knew how good Jordan was, and how dominant the Chicago Bulls had become.

After Jordan, new stars like Kobe Bryant, LeBron James, Stephen Curry and others continued to bring attention to the game, and international players like Dirk Nowitzki, Tony Parker and Yao Ming helped teams realize that talent could be found anywhere in the world.

## THE MODERN ERA

Now that you know how basketball began and evolved over the years, I'll point out some on-court differences from the way the game used to be played compared to how it's played today.

**Good Shots**

If you asked someone what they thought a "good shot" was in 1981, and someone else what they thought a "good shot" was in 2021, the answer would be completely different.

In 1981, the answer to that question would involve an attempt at the basket that came from eight feet away by one of the team's taller players.

In 2021, the answer to that question would be "the first open shot the team got."

Teams often used to use most of the shot clock in hopes of letting a star player try to put moves on his defender, or pass the ball around. Coaches would become angry when players made an attempt early in their possession, believing that if they were a little more patient, a better shot would come along later.

That thinking isn't as popular anymore, as players and coaches feel like a better shot isn't always guaranteed. It may still be smart to use up most of the time in a late game situation, but for the most part, good shooters have the green light to let it fly when they have room to do so.

## Three Point Parades

When the three-point line was introduced to the NBA in 1979, not that many players used it. As mentioned above, people were wired to think that possessions that ended with a shot closer to the basket were most desirable.

But as the years have passed, attitudes towards the three-pointer have changed. In the 1990's, teams used it a little more when they were able to make a few passes that found a player standing wide open behind the arc.

The number of attempts from "downtown" climbed a bit from 2000-2010, but they dramatically shot up starting in 2012-2013. There are a number of reasons for this, but one of the most popular theories is the 'Steph Curr-ification' of basketball.

I may have just made up a word there, but I promise my grammar is pretty good otherwise.

Curry is the greatest shooter in the history of the game by any measure, and has made a habit of swishing three-point shots from extremely far away from the basket. This has led other players to start practicing and attempting these long-range shots, and it's been commonplace ever since.

## Players Who Can and Can't Shoot

In previous eras of basketball, there were a lot of professional players who weren't good shooters. Some of those guys still exist today, but that number has decreased significantly.

In the past, players who couldn't shoot well would be valued highly for other skills they brought to the table. Maybe they were great defenders, or unselfish passers who could get their teammates open looks at the basket. Perhaps they were excellent rebounders, and were drawn to missed shots like a magnet.

Today, those skills are still appreciated, but defenses make it hard to keep on the floor players who can't shoot well. Defenses are smarter than ever, and will leave the worst shooting player wide open from the three-point line, while the player "guarding" a below average shooter helps stop another player.

Even though basketball games are supposed to be five on five, sometimes having a player who can't shoot on a team can make it seem like a four on five competition. Back in the day, teams didn't worry about this too much, but they do now.

## Post Up Play

As I said earlier, shots closer to the basket used to be viewed as a good thing, while shots taken from far away were thought of as silly.

In order to get closer shots to the basket, teams would pass the ball to a power forward or center who would try to position themselves by the thick rectangle on either side of the paint. This area is generally known as the "low post," which is where big men used to try to back their defender down to get off a close shot.

The entire objective of a possession would be to get the ball to that spot, and everything else that happened would work off the taller player with the ball.

In this day and age, you rarely see these type of post ups anymore. Players are now more spread out from one another, and are usually attempting to dribble past their man rather than back him down.

## Double Teams

Because you don't see post up plays anymore, you also don't see defenses trying to double team their opponents as much. A double team is exactly what it sounds like—two defenders try to surround the player with the ball. This is usually done to force the offensive player to panic and make a bad decision, or to simply get the basketball out of their hands and into the hands of what the defense feels is a less talented teammate.

Everyone watching, whether in the arena or on TV, knew where a post up play would take place. The defense could predictably send a double team to that area because they knew what the offense was going to do.

Now, with players so spread out, double teaming is much more difficult. Defenders have to cover a lot more ground on the court after swarming the player with the ball, and offense comes from everywhere on the floor instead of just the post up position.

**Coach Interviews During the Game**

You may not realize that NBA head coaches weren't always interviewed while the game was going on. This started within the last 10-15 years, when networks wanted to bring fans closer to the game.

Sometimes coaches do reveal their true feelings about how things are going, and other times they offer only one or two-word responses, which can be amusing to fans.

Back in the day, interviewing the coach was never even considered, as fans assumed they were too focused on trying to win and keeping their minds on the game. But this relatively new aspect has been a lot of fun, and it will probably stick around for years to come.

# 2

# HOW THE GAME IS PLAYED

Basketball looks like a ton of fun! Everyone's having a great time running up and down the court, and it's something you'd like to participate in, right?

That's music to my ears. Let's put in our Airpods and jam out to some basketball-related tunes.

While you lace up your sneakers and find your hoops shorts, I've got to fill you in on a few things. The sport is fantastic, but just as with anything else, there are things you can and can't do.

Read up on the regulations below, so you can step on to the court with a clear idea of how to play.

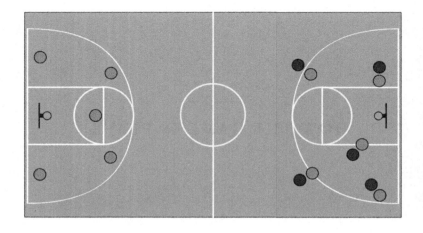

## BASIC RULES

### *Ball handlers*

Basketball is a pretty easy game to understand. The objective is to put the ball in the basket, but there are a few things to keep in mind to make sure you aren't called for a violation.

Dribbling, or bouncing the ball, is required if you have possession of the ball and are moving around the court. Once you receive the basketball, you can start dribbling at any time and move as you please around the court. But once you stop dribbling, you have to stop moving, and can take no more than two steps towards the basket after your last bounce.

If you stop dribbling and you're not intending to shoot, you must pass the ball to a teammate. The dribbling rules described above begin again for that teammate. If the ball is passed back to you, you can dribble and move with the ball again.

There's a phrase in basketball that's called "keeping your dribble alive." Of course, it's not like watering your plant or feeding your pet. Keeping your dribble alive means continuing to bounce the ball until you decide what you want to do next (pass or shoot).

When you jump with the basketball (ideally to shoot, but sometimes to pass), you cannot land with the ball still in your possession. While you're in mid-air, the ball needs to leave your hands.

### *Offensive Players Without the Ball*

If your team is on offense, but you don't have the ball, you can pretty much run around wherever you want on the court.

There's one thing to be aware of, though. There's a rectangle in front of the basket that is commonly referred to as "the paint." You get three guesses as to why that is, but you'll probably only need one.

It's usually full of color, painted with a color that matches the home team's uniform. As an offensive player, you can only stand in that area for three seconds at a time. You are welcome to visit the paint for three seconds, leave for one second, and come back in for another three, but each trip can't be more than three seconds.

If you're caught violating this rule, you can be whistled for "three in the key," and the ball goes to the other team.

***Scoring***

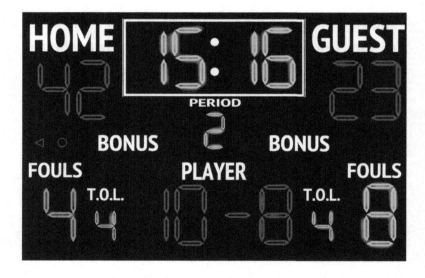

Putting the ball in the basket is the name of the game, but how much is each shot worth?

*Three points*—If your feet are behind the curved arc behind the paint and the free throw line when you take a shot, you'll be awarded three points if you make it. Because these attempts are taken the furthest from the basket, you get the most points per shot for making them. The reward is greater, but so is the difficulty.

It's important to note that if any part of your foot (yes, even that tiny pinkie toe) is on the three-point line when you shoot, the basket will count as only two points.

*Two points*—If you make a shot anywhere on the court inside of the three-point line during regular game play, the basket will be worth two points. These shots tend to make up the majority of points scored by a team, even though three pointers have become much more popular in recent history.

*One point*—If you're fouled when you have the ball on offense (more on this below), you may have the chance to take shots at the free throw line with no one guarding you. The free throw line is located at the top of the colored rectangle described earlier.

Each basket made from this area for a free throw attempt is worth one point.

### Timing

An NBA game lasts for 48 minutes, and is played with four 12-minute quarters. College basketball games last 40 minutes, and are usually played with two 20-minute halves.

Games at lower levels of basketball are shorter, with high school games usually lasting 32 minutes over four 8-minute quarters. In middle school and elementary school, quarters will usually run for five or six minutes.

In college basketball and professional basketball, a shot clock is used. It's another timer that ensures an offensive team takes at least one shot within a certain period of time. The NBA has a 24-second shot clock, and college basketball has a 30-second shot clock. The clock resets if the ball hits the rim on a shot attempt or if possession changes.

Coaches also can take timeouts throughout the course of a game to speak to their team about strategy, or stop a run of points from an opposing team. The number of timeouts available to coaches varies at each level.

## *Fouls*

We've spent a lot of time talking about offense and how it works, but there's another important element to the game. A common phrase in basketball is that "defense wins championships," and stopping the opponent is arguably just as important as putting the ball in the basket.

A good way to describe a basketball guarding position is to picture someone who doesn't want to be caught sticking their hand in the cookie jar. If your mom or dad finds you in the kitchen and asks why there are crumbs on the countertop, you'll stand straight up with both hands in the air proclaiming, "I didn't do it!"

(Be careful, they might catch you next time!)

In any event, standing with your chest pointed straight ahead and your hands above your head will keep you away from unnecessary fouls in basketball. It's when you start to reach towards the offensive player, perhaps even leaning on them or striking a part of their body with your hands or arms, that fouls are called.

In college basketball or lower levels of the game, each player is allowed to commit up to five fouls. In the NBA, each player is allowed six fouls. At any level, if a player reaches the maximum number, they are considered to be "fouled out," and cannot return to the game.

Fouls can result in the offensive player being allowed to take one, two or three free throws, which again are worth one point each.

**Important Terms to Know**

*Assist:* A pass made by a player that directly leads to a basket by one of his teammates. For example, your friend passes you the ball, and you catch it and immediately score. You get the points, and your friend gets the assist.

**Other terms for assist:** dime, helper

*Rebound:* Catching the ball after a missed shot attempt. A rebound most commonly takes place when a ball bounces off the rim, but it could happen when the basketball hits the backboard, or misses the rim entirely.

**Other terms for rebounding:** cleaning the glass, hitting the boards, 'bounding.

*Steal:* Taking the ball away from an offensive player without committing a foul.

*Other terms for steal:* picking a pocket, swipe.

*Block:* When a defensive player slaps/knocks the ball away from an offensive player while they are about to release a shot, or have already released the shot.

*Other terms for block*: rejection, stuffed, protecting the rim.

*Goaltending:* When a player tries to block a shot that an offensive player already released, but the shot is moving in a downward direction towards the basket.

*Charge:* An offensive player cannot run full speed into a defensive player. This will always result in a foul called against the offensive player. Also, if the defensive player is positioned with their hands up in front of an offensive player, and they are crashed into, a foul will be called on the offensive player.

This is one of the hardest calls for a referee to make, because they have to judge whether a defensive player was able to fully establish a stance in front of the oncoming offensive player. Even though it can be difficult to determine, it is a rule, and is called a charge.

*Double Dribble:* Remember when I said you can't dribble again once you stop? If you try to dribble again after stopping, you will be called for a double dribble and the ball will go to the other team.

*Traveling:* Similarly, if you've stopped dribbling, and you try to continue taking steps, you'll hear a whistle. This is called traveling, and the ball will go to the other team.

I also want to review the responsibilities each player has on the floor. You know that basketball continues to evolve and grow with each passing year, so some of this information is based on what players at certain positions have historically done. As you watch games moving forward, you will realize that the responsibilities can be shared amongst several players.

## Point Guard

Making short jokes might seem pretty funny to you, but it wouldn't be wise to tease your point guard about their height. They're usually the shortest players on a basketball team, but a point guard has a lot of responsibility! For starters, they're the ones who dribble the ball up the floor the most consistently, so most offensive possessions will start with the ball in their hands.

Because of this, it's important for point guards to be smart and observant when it comes to making decisions that will affect their entire team. They have the freedom to keep the ball if they believe that they will be able to get a good shot at the basket, but shooting every time is usually not wise.

The point guard is supposed to get their teammates involved, and make sure the ball is going to the player who has the best chance to score.

On defense, they will also be tasked with trying to make life difficult for the opposing point guard, who will also be trying to smoothly start his team's offensive possession.

**Shooting Guard**

This might sound like the most fun position to play on a basketball team. Shooting guard—that means you get to shoot all you want, right? Bombs away!

Yes and no. It's true that a shooting guard is generally expected to be the most skilled player on the team at scoring points, and it's essential for them to be able to consistently make jump shots. It's also helpful if a shooting guard has solid dribbling ability. They may not be as good as a point guard at handling the ball, but they should be good enough to take the ball to the basket around a defender.

Sounds like a pretty sweet deal, right? It is, but there are other things this player has to do as well.

Shooting guards often have to run around the court more than the other players, and are often the main target of an opposing defense. This makes sense, because if a team knows that a shooting guard is the best scorer, they will try to stop them from making easy baskets. As a result, a shooting guard needs to be in excellent physical shape, as they cannot afford to get tired when a shot has to be made.

While a shooting guard generally has the green light to take shots, it's important that they don't take bad shots. For example, if a shooting guard is leaning away from the basket, with two players guarding him, shooting may not be the best idea. Another player on the court might be more open than the shooting guard in that situation, so they should pass the ball if there's time to do so.

**Small Forward**

Have you ever heard the term "Jack of All Trades"? You might think this refers to a boy named Jack, who was skilled at trading bad sweets for the good stuff at lunch in the cafeteria.

But the term actually refers to someone who is good or talented at many things. The player who comes closest to being a "Jack of All Trades" on the basketball court is the small forward.

A small forward's height is usually the median (pay attention in math class!) of his teammates. Because they're not the smallest but also not the tallest player, they have the ability to contribute in many different ways.

For example, if the point guard wants a break from dribbling the ball up the floor, a skilled small forward might be able to cover for them once in a while. They can also help out by scoring themselves, or by rebounding the ball.

Perhaps a small forward's biggest impact comes on defense, though. They should be able to guard the opposing small forward, but are also not in a bad spot if they need to switch to defending a shorter or taller player. This can be extremely valuable during the course of a game.

Even if a small forward isn't the best player on the court at any one skill, they should be able to respectably fill in where needed when called upon.

## Power Forward

As we continue our trek through a basketball lineup in size order, our next stop brings us to the power forward. The name of this position might be a little confusing, since basketball doesn't seem like a game where power would be needed. If it was, we would need to buy a helmet and shoulder pads, right?

But strength and toughness is important in basketball, especially as you get closer to the basket. That's where you'll find taller players like the power forward, who are actively using their lower bodies to try and move opponents out of position on defense.

Power forwards are also expected to be a force in the rebounding department, and to prevent opposing teams from having multiple chances to score a basket.

That's where a little bit of grit and determination comes in handy. There are a bunch of hands, arms and bodies swarming to the basketball after a missed shot, and a power forward is tasked with overcoming all of them to come down with the ball.

Offensively, power forwards traditionally have been the least skilled players on the floor, although that has changed in recent basketball history. Back in the day, it would be surprising for a power forward to take and make a shot from more than 15 feet away, since their job was to stay close to the basket. In this day and age, however, power forwards have extended their range considerably, and can make three-point shots just like smaller players.

**Center**

Hopefully you're in a comfortable spot while reading this book, but we may have to adjust our necks a little bit as we look up at the player in the center position. They're usually the tallest on the court, and have been known to duck under the top of door frames so they don't hit their heads. There's a hilarious scene in *Space Jam* where former NBA center Shawn Bradley smacks his head on the ceiling—check it out!

Our vertically gifted friends can affect a game in multiple ways. They are usually pretty adept at scoring close to the basket, and can attempt different types of shots without the fear of being blocked. Because they usually shoot close to the basket, the percentage of shots they make is usually greater than players at other positions.

They're also used as "screeners" or are asked to "set the pick" in a pick and roll situation. This is a basketball play where a teammate runs to a spot and stands still, keeping his arms within the frame of his body. The ball handler will "use the pick," which will slow his defender down as the defensive player either runs into or around the screener. Centers are usually the biggest players, which is why it makes sense for them to be screeners.

On defense, a center has one of the most important jobs in the game. They are assigned to the other center, and will need to make sure that they don't get chances to score easy shots. Centers are also responsible for helping their teammates by challenging opposing teams' shots at the basket. Even if a center cannot block a shot, getting in front of a player and putting their arms up can make a shot at the basket much more difficult.

Just like with power forwards, the expectations and skill levels for centers have changed and evolved over the years. Centers' defensive responsibilities have not changed that much, but their offensive jump shooting range has, as well as their ability to dribble the basketball.

# 3

# THE GREATEST OF ALL TIME

We've reached that point in the book where it's time to talk about GOATS. Wait, what? *What do farm animals have to do with basketball?* you might be asking yourself.

The answer is nothing. While you might come across a goat during a school field trip to the zoo, I'm talking about a completely different kind of GOAT. These are the human kind, and don't make noise when they want to be fed (in most cases).

In the last few years, GOAT has come to stand for "Greatest of All Time," and is commonly used in sports to give the very best players their proper respect.

The GOATs made their mark in the game of basketball by winning championships, scoring a lot of points, making their teammates better, and playing great defense. They're extremely famous NBA players whose talent and skill rose above most of their peers. They also loved the game more than anything else, and worked extremely hard to continue getting better and better.

But there's another thing that all of these players have in common. Any guesses?

They were once all children with dreams about what they wanted to be when they grew up. The path to greatness wasn't always easy, but they continued to believe in themselves every step of the way.

Let's learn a little bit more about the 10 players who rank as the greatest of all time.

**Magic Johnson**

**Full Name:** Earvin Johnson Jr.
**Nickname:** Magic
**Born:** August 14, 1959
**Hometown:** Lansing, Michigan
**College:** Michigan State
**Year Turned Pro:** 1979
**Total NBA Seasons:** 13
**Height:** 6'9"
**Position:** Point Guard
**NBA Team:** Los Angeles Lakers #32
**Notable Quote:**

---

*"Ask not what your teammates can do for you. Ask what you can do for your teammates."*

---

There may not be a happier player in NBA history than Magic Johnson. If your parents let you watch YouTube or social media and you can pull up old video of Magic, you'll see that he was always smiling!

But life wasn't always full of sunshine and roses for the man everyone called Magic. He had nine brothers and sisters, and his parents worked really hard to make sure they had food on the table every night. Young Earvin didn't have TikTok to showcase his vocal skills, but he would pass the time singing in the neighborhood with his friends.

When he wasn't busting out a tune, Magic would obsess over the game of basketball, even when he couldn't get to a hoop. On his way to the convenience store on cold Michigan days, he would dribble his ball with his right and left hand. While most kids sleep next to stuffed animals or action figures, Magic would snuggle up to his basketball when he went to bed each night, like it was a teddy bear.

His love for the sport would continue as he attended Everett High School, and later, Michigan State University. Magic had a wonderful college career, which ended with him leading the Michigan State Spartans to a national championship in 1979.

Because of his accomplishments in college, he was already a popular player before he entered the NBA. The Lakers were lucky enough to have the first pick in the NBA Draft in 1979, and Magic's exciting brand of basketball seemed like a perfect fit for them.

There was one major question though. The Lakers' best player when Johnson arrived was Kareem Abdul-Jabbar, a center who played close to the basket. Johnson loved to push the ball up and down the court on the fast break. Would the two stars get along and play well together?

The answer would come in the Lakers' very first game. Abdul-Jabbar would make a shot at the buzzer to defeat the San Diego Clippers, and Magic jumped into his arms in celebration, as if he was his best friend. It was clear from that moment forward that both players were willing to work together to win championships.

One of Magic's most special moments came in the 1980 NBA Finals, in his first year as a player. Abdul-Jabbar was forced to miss the game in which Los Angeles had a chance to clinch the championship, and the Lakers had to decide who to replace him with at the center position. The head coach decided that Johnson, their 6'9" point guard, would be the best choice.

It turned out to be the right move. Magic had one of the best games of his career, totaling 42 points, 15 rebounds and seven assists. Because of him, the Lakers would go on to win the title!

It was this type of unselfishness that made Magic one of the greatest players in NBA history, and so successful over the course of his career. He would grab a rebound, push the ball up the floor and willingly pass it to the teammate who had the best opportunity to score.

Knowing this would motivate his teammates to sprint down the court next to him.

Magic would lead the Lakers to four more NBA championships in the 1980's, making the Los Angeles Lakers a dynasty. One of his other iconic moments came in the 1987 Finals against the Boston Celtics. With only seven seconds left in the game, Johnson hit a running hook shot that gave Los Angeles a victory that would help them win the title a few days later.

Magic Johnson's basketball career in the NBA ended a little early because of an illness, but despite the setback, he would still be a part of two unique basketball experiences that are part of his legacy.

Despite not playing in an NBA game during the 1991-92 regular season, Johnson was voted into the 1992 NBA All Star Game by the fans. He would put on a show with a memorable performance, as he led the Western Conference to a victory and became the All Star Game MVP.

Magic was also invited to be on what many fans consider to be the greatest basketball team ever put together. As part of the 1992 Dream Team, Magic Johnson's talents were on full display for basketball fans all over the world, as the United States team brought home the gold medal in the Olympics.

Even after his basketball career ended, Johnson remained famous and heavily involved with the Lakers. He has served as their coach and president of basketball operations at different stages of his life. He has also been a sports commentator on TV, sharing his thoughts and viewpoints on current players and teams.

As if Magic was not already cemented as a Los Angeles legend, he was also part of a group that purchased the Los Angeles Dodgers, the city's baseball team!

**Michael Jordan**

**Full Name:** Michael Jeffrey Jordan
**Nickname:** His Airness
**Born:** February 17, 1963
**Hometown:** Brooklyn, New York
**College:** North Carolina
**Year Turned Pro:** 1984
**Total NBA Seasons:** 15
**Height:** 6'6"
**Position:** Shooting Guard
**NBA Teams:** Chicago Bulls #23, Washington Wizards #45
**Notable Quote:**

---

*"I can accept failure, everyone fails at something. But I can't accept not trying."*

---

"Like Mike... if I could be like Mike!" Those were some of the catchy lyrics to the theme song, "Be Like Mike" in a Gatorade commercial featuring Michael Jordan, and a bunch of kids who wanted to be like the Chicago Bulls star.

Before he had such a large fanbase amongst young people, Jordan was just a kid himself growing up in New York and later North Carolina. He was a normal boy who loved to play sports, but also didn't like to study that much. When he started high school, he became more focused on his classes, while also dedicating time to the game he loved so much.

While he was a sophomore at Laney High School, Jordan would be told that he wasn't good enough at basketball. Yes, you read that right. One of the greatest players in basketball history, and in sports, did not make the cut for his high school varsity team.

A lot of teenagers would have stopped playing the game if that had happened to them. They might go home and feel sad, or blame the coach for not realizing how good they were. But Michael Jordan decided to continue to work on his game so he could be ready to try out again as a junior.

He would make the team the following year, and average 25 points per game in his two years on the varsity squad.

His excellent play in his final years of high school attracted the attention of the University of North Carolina coaching staff, who were excited to keep Jordan close to where he grew up. As a member of the

Tar Heels basketball program, Jordan would display great athleticism against other college players. Most people know Jordan from his incredible play in the NBA, but he also made one of the biggest shots in NCAA basketball history.

In the 1982 championship game against Georgetown, Jordan would receive the ball in the corner, and nail a game winning jump shot to clinch the title for North Carolina.

Number 23 would enter the NBA in 1984, immediately showing other-worldly talent as a Chicago Bull. While Jordan quickly became one of the best players in the league, his team struggled to win in the playoffs.

He would still have the chance to wow fans all over the United States and around the world with his physical abilities. Jordan would dazzle basketball die-hards in a few Slam Dunk Contests, which showcased the best athletes in the league. In 1987, he took off from the free throw line and jammed it home, which is one of the farthest leaps any player has ever taken in dunk contest history.

As the 1980's came to a close, there was only one thing missing on Jordan's elite resume; an NBA title. He would end up achieving that dream for the first time in 1991, as he led the Bulls to a championship over Magic

Johnson's Lakers. Jordan would end up playing in five more NBA Finals, winning every time. His performances would deny titles to other great players like Clyde Drexler, Charles Barkley, Gary Payton, Karl Malone and John Stockton.

The six-time champion would bring the popularity of the NBA to new heights in the 1990's, which helped the league become more famous in different parts of the world. Many of the international stars we watch in today's NBA started playing basketball because they'd watched Jordan as children.

He also became more popular with children after the 1996 film he starred in called *Space Jam*. Playing on a team with Bugs Bunny, Daffy Duck, Yosemite Sam and many other Looney Tunes, Jordan encouraged and trained the cartoon characters to beat the evil squad known as the Monstars, who stole the talent of NBA players.

What makes Jordan's accomplishments even more impressive is that he left the NBA for nearly two years when he was at the peak of his abilities in order to play professional baseball for the Birmingham Barons. Of course, he eventually returned to the Bulls to win more rings.

The star shooting guard would retire from the game in 1998... but it would not be for good. In fact, Jordan ended up working in the front office for the Washington Wizards, which meant he was able to pick who would play on the team, and in 2001, Jordan joined the Wizards on the court!

Even though he was pushing 40, Jordan showed he could still play with the young guys. He made two more All-Star teams while he played for Washington.

After his time in Washington, Jordan bought the Charlotte Bobcats (now the Charlotte Hornets) in 2010. He is often seen sitting courtside at their games. Naturally, the players always want to play their best in front of the basketball legend!

**LeBron James**

**Full Name:** LeBron Raymone James
**Nickname:** King James
**Born:** December 30, 1984
**Hometown:** Akron, Ohio
**College:** Entered NBA Straight from High School
**Year Turned Pro:** 2003
**Total NBA Seasons**: 20 (and counting!)
**Height:** 6'9"
**Position:** Small Forward
**NBA Teams:** Cleveland Cavaliers #6, Miami Heat, Los Angeles Lakers #23
**Notable Quote:**

---

*"Basketball is my passion, I love it. But my family and friends mean everything to me. That's what's important. I need my phone so I can keep in contact with them at all times."*

---

Most of the GOAT's that you'll read about in this book were identified at a young age for their special basketball talent. However, only a couple of them grew up in the era of smart phones and social media, which means that fans across the country and the globe could take video of their every move.

LeBron James has had the spotlight on him ever since he was a teenager. He made the cover of *Sports Illustrated* magazine as a 17-year-old, with the title "The Chosen One" on the side of his picture. There are so many times in sports that teenagers are expected to become legends before they've ever played a professional game. In the case of James, however, those expectations were realized.

Before he became the best player in the NBA, LeBron and his mother Gloria had to deal with some challenges. When young LeBron was just five years old, he and his mom had to move five times in one year. Imagine packing up your Xbox, favorite jerseys, iPad, posters and everything else you own five times in a single year. It would be really hard!

James was determined to overcome those hardships and ultimately became one of the best basketball prospects in decades. His games at St. Vincent-St. Mary's High School were on ESPN for everyone to watch, and it seemed like destiny that he would be the next great NBA star.

It is quite rare for players to become great close to where they grew up, but James would start his NBA career with the Cleveland Cavaliers, not far from his hometown of Akron, Ohio. It was easy for his friends and family to watch him play, which made the jump from high school to the pros a little bit easier for him. He was also already used to playing games on TV, so he didn't feel too much added pressure when he joined the NBA.

Within a couple of years, the Cavaliers became one of the main attractions in the NBA, thanks to James. In 2007, when fans were not yet expecting Cleveland to contend, 22-year-old James led the team all the way to the NBA Finals. The team was swept by the San Antonio Spurs and fellow GOAT Tim Duncan, but the future for James and his teammates was extremely bright.

The Cavaliers would get very close to making the NBA Finals again during the next couple of seasons, but would fall short. In 2010, James' contract with the team was over, and he could choose to play for whatever team he wanted. Most of the teams in the league tried to persuade him to sign with them, but in the end, he chose to play for the Miami Heat. This allowed him to play with his friends Dwyane Wade and Chris Bosh.

The Heat would end up winning two championships while Lebron was on the team. He learned from Wade and Miami Heat president Pat Riley what it took to win a title. James would realize how to take over games when his team needed him to, while also deferring to his teammates when they were playing well. These were lessons that would serve him well for the rest of his career.

When James left Cleveland to play for Miami, his hometown was disappointed and saddened by the local Ohio kid's decision to leave. It did not seem like they would forgive him. But LeBron, after accomplishing his ultimate goal with the Heat, was looking for his next challenge, and in 2014 he returned to the Cavaliers, who now had some new young talented players on the roster, like Kyrie Irving and Tristan Thompson.

The Cavaliers were one of the few teams in the NBA that had never won a championship, but James put his heart and soul into changing that fact. In the 2016 NBA Finals, Cleveland was down three games to one to the Golden State Warriors, and it seemed like they were going to lose again. The Cavaliers never gave up, though, and forced a Game 7. In Game 7, James would block Warriors forward Andre Iguodala's shot from behind, and this single move completely changed the momentum of the game. Kyrie Irving would make a three pointer after that to give the Cavaliers the win, and their first NBA championship!

LeBron would ultimately make yet another move—this time, out west. He signed with the Los Angeles Lakers in hopes of continuing his quest to win more championships. The Lakers would send a lot of their good young players and draft picks to the New Orleans Pelicans to receive Anthony Davis, who was one of the best big men in the NBA. Together, Davis and James were magnificent during a playoff run in 2020, which led to the Lakers winning the NBA title. This ring would be James' fourth.

King James is still with the Lakers, and is hoping to achieve more team and individual success. The small forward is looking to break the all-time scoring record held by Kareem Abdul-Jabbar.

James is also enjoying being a father, and watching his sons, Bronny and Bryce, chart their own basketball journey in Southern California.

## Tim Duncan

**Full Name:** Timothy Theodore Duncan
**Nickname:** The Big Fundamental
**Born:** April 25, 1976
**Hometown:** St. Croix, U.S. Virgin Islands
**College:** Wake Forest
**Year Turned Pro:** 1997
**Total NBA Seasons:** 19
**Height:** 6'11"
**Position:** Power Forward
**NBA Team:** San Antonio Spurs #21
**Notable Quote:**

---

*"I enjoy jokes, smiling, and making people smile. I may be a little different, but that's OK, who wants to be normal anyway?"*

---

It may seem hard to believe, but Tim Duncan became one of the greatest basketball players of all time by accident. Most of his childhood was not spent dreaming about the sport, or how he would go on to have one of the most decorated NBA careers in history.

That's because Duncan spent the majority of his early years in a pool.

That's right! Instead of lacing up basketball sneakers and putting on basketball shorts, Duncan was walking around the Virgin Islands in his flip flips and swim trunks. There were days he would swim close to five miles. Enter that distance into your computer or smartphone, and you will quickly realize that it's a very long way to swim!

Unfortunately for Duncan, his childhood dreams of excelling in water sports were dashed by Hurricane Hugo, which destroyed the main pool where he trained. He was already a natural athlete in fantastic shape, so he had to find another sport to focus on. When he was 14 years old, he began to play basketball.

This was going to be an interesting experiment, to say the least. Duncan was obviously tall, but he had very little prior experience to fall back on. He did not have a youth coach or mentor who taught him drills when he was in elementary or middle school. Duncan would have to catch up quickly, but he was extremely intelligent and observant.

In an unlikely turn of events, the boy from St. Croix would turn himself into a legitimate player, one that noted college basketball programs in the continental

United States were interested in. Wake Forest University in North Carolina did a lot of homework on the evolving post player, and were amazed by what he could do, considering he had only been playing the sport for a couple of years.

The Demon Deacons coaching staff wasted little time getting Duncan into their lineup. He started 32 games as a freshman, and averaged 10 points and 10 rebounds. What was even scarier for opponents was that he averaged nearly four blocks per game in his first college season, which made it very hard to score on Wake Forest.

As his college career progressed, Duncan's ability to score improved, as he would make baskets on the box next to the painted area, and make bank shots that hit the backboard before going through the hoop.

His offensive ability and his defensive prowess made him an attractive player to the NBA. The San Antonio Spurs already had an All-Star big man in David Robinson, and usually NBA teams like to add players in areas where their current players are not that good. However, the Spurs realized how special Duncan was, and believed that he and Robinson would find a way to play well together.

San Antonio was absolutely right. When Duncan first joined the team, and it was clear that he could play well with Robinson, the two players were nicknamed "The Twin Towers." Scoring at the rim was very difficult for teams with the 6'11" Duncan and the 7'1" Robinson ready to jump.

After finishing with one of the NBA's worst records in the season before they added Duncan, the Spurs transformed into one of the league's best squads. During the 1998-1999 season, San Antonio made somewhat of a surprising run to the NBA Finals, where they squared off against the New York Knicks. The Spurs had a lot of experienced players on that team, but relied on their young star to deliver during the biggest games of the season. Duncan did just that, and his play led the team to the title, and earned him the NBA Finals MVP award.

It would have been easy for Duncan to think more about himself and seek out even more attention as one of the best NBA players at such a young age. Instead, the quiet superstar remained humble, and always spoke about the team first, and what they could do better. When San Antonio brought international stars Manu Ginobili and Tony Parker onto the team, Duncan was delighted to help them improve so the team could get back to winning more championships.

With a potent big three, the Spurs would again win titles in 2003, 2005 and 2007. Even though they were dominant, they didn't receive a lot of press from the media... but that's precisely how Duncan liked it.

After their 2007 title, it did not appear that the Spurs would make another run at the championship. Duncan was getting older, and there were many other talented teams in their conference.

Then in 2013, San Antonio made it back to the Finals, and were within seconds of winning a title against the Miami Heat. However, a miraculous shot by Heat guard Ray Allen forced a Game 7, and Miami managed to secure the trophy that year.

The following season, San Antonio was determined to win the title, thinking that they'd let a golden opportunity slip away the year before. They won 62 regular season games, and earned a rematch with the Heat in the 2014 Finals. This time, the Spurs completely blitzed Miami, and won the title, the fifth of Duncan's illustrious career.

Duncan would retire in 2016, and not surprisingly, he would stay out of the spotlight. He did briefly become an assistant coach for the Spurs, because of his strong relationship with head coach Gregg Popovich, but soon returned to private life away from the bright lights.

## Kareem Abdul-Jabbar

**Full Name:** Kareem Abdul-Jabbar (born Ferdinand Lewis Alcindor Jr.)
**Nickname:** Big Fella
**Born:** April 16, 1947
**Hometown:** New York, New York
**College:** UCLA
**Year Turned Pro:** 1969
**Total NBA Seasons:** 20
**Height:** 7'2"
**Position:** Center
**NBA Teams:** Milwaukee Bucks #33, Los Angeles Lakers #3
**Notable Quote:**

---

*"One man can be a crucial ingredient to a team, but one man cannot make a team."*

---

When you look at the record book of achievements in NBA history, one of the most impressive numbers you'll ever see is 38,387. What does that number signify, you ask? That is the number of total points Kareem Abdul-Jabbar scored in his NBA career. It's the most points any player has ever scored in league history.

Think about that for a second. How many shots do you take when you play basketball at the park or your local gym? On a good day, you're probably playing with your buddies for a few hours, and do a lot of shooting during that time. But can you ever imagine making 15,837 two-point shots? How about 6,712 free throws?

That's how many shots it took Abdul-Jabbar to score all of his points (except for three), and it took him a long time to get to that number. He played in the NBA for 20 years, which is probably around twice the amount of time you've been alive!

A lot happened in Abdul-Jabbar's life before he became the NBA's career leader in scoring. He was born with a different name, Lew Alcindor, in New York City. He was a tall boy who was determined to learn from wise older people and follow his love of basketball. This helped divert his attention from the troubles his family experienced. For example, sometimes his mom couldn't afford to buy everything she needed for her family. Because of such financial difficulties, life was often sad for her and her young son Lew.

During high school, Lew became one of the most dominant players in the entire country. Everyone wanted to

know where he would play basketball when he graduated. It was important to him to find a college program
that would help him improve on the court, but would
also teach him important life lessons and challenge his
brain.

Many people thought he would end up playing college
basketball in New York, but Alcindor ended up
choosing a school far away, in Los Angeles, California.
UCLA had a strong program, and Lew really felt a
connection with head coach John Wooden. Wooden
would teach Alcindor skills on the court, but wanted to
pass on other knowledge as well that would help him
for the rest of his life.

It turned out to be a great decision. The UCLA Bruins
only lost two games during the three years the young
center was with the team, and they won the college
championship every single season. For his college
career, Alcindor averaged over 26 points and 15
rebounds per game.

He had one of the best college careers of all time, and
every NBA team would've loved to have him when he
left school, but it was the Milwaukee Bucks that ended
up drafting him in 1969. They really lucky,
because they could pair him with Oscar Robertson,
who was also one of the best players in NBA history.

Shortly after joining the NBA, Alcindor would officially change his name to Kareem Abdul-Jabbar. It did not matter what his name was, or what people thought of him, as Abdul-Jabbar proved right away that he was going to go down in history as a special player. In just his second year as a professional, Abdul-Jabbar and Robertson led the Bucks to an NBA championship. It's not easy for a young player to be one of the best, but Abdul-Jabbar clearly was!

Abdul-Jabbar would end up playing six seasons for Milwaukee, and then spent the final 14 years of his NBA career with the Los Angeles Lakers. When Magic Johnson joined the team in 1979, the two would form one of the greatest duos in NBA history. Abdul-Jabbar would win five more championships in Los Angeles.

Now that you know more about Abdul-Jabbar's background, let's return to all those points he scored. How was he able to accomplish that? After all, he only made one three-pointer in 20 NBA seasons, so he was only adding to his total one or two points at a time.

The answer is that he had a secret weapon… a shot that no one before Abdul-Jabbar or anyone who played after him has ever mastered. It was called the sky hook.

Already tall, standing 7'2", Abdul-Jabbar's sky hook shot made him pretty much unstoppable. After a few dribbles, he would take the ball in one of his large hands, and then spin the ball towards the basketball with his super long fingers. The ball would go high in the air towards the sky, and gently fall into the hoop.

It was a beautiful shot, and it helped Abdul-Jabbar remain a threat to opposing teams even as he was in his final NBA seasons.

Now go ahead and count to 38,387... after you finish reading the book, of course.

**Kobe Bryant**

**Full Name:** Kobe Bean Bryant
**Nickname:** Black Mamba
**Born:** August 23, 1978
**Hometown:** Philadelphia, Pennsylvania
**College:** Entered NBA Straight from High School
**Year Turned Pro:** 1996
**Total NBA Seasons:** 20
**Height:** 6'6"
**Position:** Shooting Guard
**NBA Team:** Los Angeles Lakers #8 & #24
**Notable Quote:**

---

*"Sports are such a great teacher. I think of everything they've taught me: camaraderie, humility, how to resolve differences."*

---

When you go by only one name, you know you've accomplished something great. Add Kobe to that list. Kobe Bryant was one of the best shooting guards in NBA history. He had a desire to be the best, and was willing to put in a lot of work to accomplish his dreams. When other people were sleeping, eating or goofing off, Kobe was in the gym exercising or practicing basketball.

There was no guarantee that Kobe Bryant would ever become one of the greatest basketball players of all time. As a boy, change was one of the only constants in his life. What if you had to go to a new school without much warning, and make new friends without saying goodbye to your old ones?

That was Kobe's life for much of his childhood, as his family moved to follow his father's professional basketball career. There was even a short time when young Kobe lived in Italy. Not only did he have to make new friends; he had to learn a new language just to be able to speak with other kids.

Moving so often was not easy, but it taught Kobe to be flexible, and to learn how to succeed in different types of situations. He and his family would eventually make their way back to the United States, and Kobe would be a popular high school player at Lower Merion High School near Philadelphia. The NBA was interested in him during high school, and how good he could be even without playing college basketball.

It is not always smart to skip college, but Bryant did that, and it worked out for him. He was acquired by the

Los Angeles Lakers in the 1996 NBA Draft, which is where he would spend his entire career.

You might know that Kobe won five championships in his career with the Lakers, or that he was one of the greatest players to have on your team when the game was close and you needed a basket. But you might not know that performing in the clutch didn't always work out for him.

Before Los Angeles became one of the best teams in NBA history from 2000-2003, Bryant had to go through some growing pains. The Lakers would lose in the playoffs, and Bryant badly airballed a shot against the Utah Jazz one year, which left people wondering if he would ever become a great player.

There were no more doubts about that after the 2000 NBA Finals, as Kobe put on a show in one of the most important games of the series. Fellow superstar Shaquille O'Neal fouled out of Game 4, and someone else needed to step up to carry the team to victory. Enter the 21-year-old Bryant, who was not afraid of the moment. He was spectacular in the final moments of the game, and the Lakers would go on to win the title thanks to his efforts.

The reason the Lakers were so amazing during that time was because Bryant's skills improved, but also because he learned how to be a better teammate. At first, it wasn't always easy for him to play with O'Neal, who preferred to play the game a little more slowly than Bryant. However, through communication and a shared goal of winning, the two greats were able to come to an understanding, and the results spoke for themselves.

During the course of his career, Bryant proved that he would do whatever it took to help his team win. He is known for his exceptional scoring, but was also named as one of the top defenders in the NBA in 12 different seasons! He had a great ability to move his feet, and keep the offensive player he was guarding in front of him. Bryant would give maximum effort jumping to try and make the offensive player's attempt to score more difficult.

Remember I mentioned that Kobe had to learn Italian back when he was kid? He also learned Spanish as an adult, so he could communicate with teammates and opponents. This came in handy when speaking to one of his favorite teammates later in his career, Pau Gasol.

The Lakers were not the best team in the last couple years of Bryant's career, but he finished his legendary stint in the NBA with one final game that everyone remembers. Against the Utah Jazz, the same team against which he'd shot the airballs early in his career, Bryant finished with 60 points in the last game he would ever play in the NBA. All of his friends, family and former teammates were at the game to cheer him on, and pay their respects to one of the best players to ever play the game.

**Stephen Curry**

**Full Name:** Wardell Stephen Curry II
**Nicknames**: Steph, Chef Curry
**Born:** March 14, 1988
**Hometown:** Akron, Ohio
**College:** Davidson
**Year Turned Pro:** 2009
**Total NBA Seasons:** 13 (and counting!)
**Height:** 6'2"
**Position:** Point Guard
**NBA Team:** Golden State Warriors #30
**Notable Quote:**

---

*"I try to make it look easy, but the behind-the-scenes stuff is the challenge."*

---

L et's pick up Stephen Curry's story right from his own words in the above notable quote. To say he makes playing the game of basketball look easy might be the understatement of the century.

You don't even need to watch him play in a game to understand just how "Stephortless" the sport is for him. Pay attention to the type of shots he takes in warmups and pregame. There has arguably been no player who fans have wanted to show up early to watch *practice* more than Curry.

He routinely connects on shots from half-court that are extremely challenging for other professionals. On certain layups, Curry tosses the ball very high in the air, almost like he's just playing around... only for it to come straight down into the hoop. He'll also make long distance shots while sitting on the bench, or while standing in the tunnel entrance players walk through to get to the court.

It truly is remarkable, as his game feels like an actual performance, and his stage is the basketball court and everything around it.

It's fair to say that Curry feels at home on an NBA court because he's spent so much time on it, both as a child and as an adult. He is the son of Dell Curry, who played 16 years in the league, and would let his sons shoot with professionals when they were young boys. There are a lot of really cool pictures of Steph as a kid sitting next to NBA stars of the 1990's and 2000's.

Stephen Curry would have a lot of fun playing basketball as a child, but was also smart enough to speak with his dad and his teammates about the best way to succeed in the sport. This was a unique thing, as Curry was trying to learn by watching the game just as much as he was improving with a basketball in his hands.

It was pretty clear that Curry was always going to be able to shoot the ball, but there was concern that his body was not strong enough to compete against other players. Even though his frame was slender, Curry was still able to put up points at every level he played at. When he was 12 years old, he used a move that his coach wanted to teach adults. This level of skill and prowess with the basketball allowed him to overcome his skinny build.

Even though he had an amazing high school career in the Charlotte area, a lot of the powerhouse basketball college programs did not want to take a chance on the small-ish guard. But one university welcomed him with open arms, and Curry proved to the world that he was one of the best players in the country.

While attending Davidson College in North Carolina, the future NBA star consistently drained three-pointers from distances most players would not even consider attempting. It didn't really matter that he didn't look as sturdy as other players—as long as he had a little bit of space to shoot, there was an excellent chance he would score.

During the 2008 March Madness college basketball tournament, Curry made a dazzling display of shots that put him on the map. Because of his stellar play, Davidson was beating some of the best teams in the nation, which many college basketball fans were very surprised about.

When he announced he was leaving Davidson to enter the NBA Draft, there were still questions even then about how he would hold up playing against grown men. But the Golden State Warriors saw enough from the Davidson guard to choose him in the 2009 NBA Draft, and the rest is history.

There were a couple of years early in his career where Curry battled ankle injuries, but he would overcome them to show that his skill set is amongst the most potent in league history.

There are two things that most people will remember about Curry even after he retires from the NBA. There is no doubt that he is the greatest shooter of all time, as he drains long distance shots both off the dribble and standing still. There hasn't been anyone who has even come close to Curry in terms of the amount of three-pointers he's made in his career. Curry set the all-time record for three-pointers in 2021 against the New York Knicks. Ray Allen had the record before Curry, and was there to congratulate him and give him a hug.

The second accomplishment of Curry's career that will never be forgotten are the four championships he has won (so far). Before the Warriors started their dynasty in the middle of the 2010's, there were very few teams that had ever won a title by primarily shooting a bunch of jump shots. Golden State was so good at doing that, though, that it didn't matter that they weren't always close to the basket when they tried to score.

There have been and will continue to be great players who play at the NBA level, but arguably no one player has changed the sport more than Curry. Other players and children now have the confidence to shoot from great distances because Curry does, which has made the three-point shot more of a factor than it ever was before.

## Shaquille O'Neal

**Full Name:** Shaquille Rashaun O'Neal
**Nickname:** Diesel
**Born:** March 6, 1972
**Hometown:** Newark, New Jersey
**College:** LSU
**Year Turned Pro:** 1992
**Total NBA Seasons:** 19
**Height:** 7'1"
**Position:** Center
**NBA Teams:** Orlando Magic #32, Los Angeles Lakers #34, Miami Heat #32, Phoenix Suns #2, Cleveland Cavaliers #33, Boston Celtics #36
**Notable Quote:**

*"I never worry about the problem. I worry about the solution."*

Shaquille O'Neal deserves to make this respected list of GOATs because of his stellar NBA career, but he also has one of the most entertaining personalities of any athlete. When the game was on the line and plays had to be made, O'Neal was always locked in on what needed to be done. But before the game started, and even after it was over, his trademark grin and never-ending jokes entertained everyone and ensured people thought well of him.

Today, O'Neal is known for the commercials he does, and for his contributions to TNT's pre-game, halftime and postgame coverage of NBA games. He and Charles Barkley always seem to make each other laugh, or throw playful jabs at one another. And even though he is best known for his accolades in the world of basketball, he also has many fans outside of the sports world as well.

For as goofy a guy as he can appear to be sometimes, Shaq grew up with a lot of rules and discipline that helped him become one of the most dominant basketball players ever. He credits his stepfather for keeping him on track and showing him how to build good habits and stay away from things that can prevent kids from achieving their dreams.

There were times when Shaq did not like the amount of structure placed on him, and was not happy with his stepfather. It didn't seem fair that other kids had more freedom than he did. But as an adult, Shaq was extremely thankful for the blueprint of how to become a successful person, and admitted he probably wouldn't have achieved his goal of being a basketball player if it hadn't been for those rules.

Shaquille O'Neal is a large man, so it makes sense that he was a sizeable boy as well. He would play to his strength, literally, by using his backside to back down smaller players until he was at the rim. Even though he was taller and stronger than many of his opponents as a child, O'Neal was also very athletic. When he kept in peak shape, O'Neal was able to beat his opponents down the court and finish with rim-rattling dunks.

He would go on to play college basketball at Louisiana State University, where he put up some mind-boggling statistics. He averaged over 24 points, five blocks and 14 rebounds per game when he was a sophomore and junior at LSU. Talk about getting the job done on both ends of the floor!

It wasn't all that difficult for NBA teams to envision what Shaquille O'Neal would look like on an NBA court, because he was already a full-grown man in college. The NBA centers who played the game at the time were much more methodical and plodding, whereas O'Neal liked to run and jump as if he was a small forward.

The Orlando Magic selected O'Neal with the very first pick of the 1992 NBA Draft, meaning they felt he was the best player available that year. He came in right away and proved he belonged, and was named the NBA Rookie of The Year in the 1992-1993 season.

During that year, he also did something that would be watched over and over again for many years. He dunked the ball ferociously in a game against the New Jersey Nets, and the entire backboard was brought to the ground! While this ended up stopping the game for several minutes, it was a sign of O'Neal's unbelievable strength.

After a few magnificent years with the Magic, O'Neal joined the Los Angeles Lakers, where he would have the best seasons of his NBA career. He learned many lessons during his time in Orlando, and that experience helped him become a champion in Los Angeles.

He made the NBA Finals in 1995 with Orlando, but the team was swept against a much more prepared Houston Rockets squad. O'Neal would not let that happen to him again, and was laser-focused when the Lakers made it to the Finals in 2000, 2001 and 2002. Led by the big fella, the Lakers would win the title each of those years, staking their claim as one of the best basketball teams in NBA history. O'Neal and Kobe Bryant would also form one of the best tandems the game has ever seen.

Los Angeles made it to the NBA Finals again in 2004, but lost to the Detroit Pistons. After that, the Lakers decided to build the team around Kobe, and Shaq was traded to the Miami Heat. Many wondered whether O'Neal's best days were behind him, or if he could help transform the Heat into a legitimate title contender.

It turned out that O'Neal (nicknamed The Diesel) had a lot of gas left in the tank. In his second season in Miami, he provided the physicality in the painted area of the court that the team needed, while still being able to pour in points at the rim. He also offered leadership to a team that had been entrusted to the young Dwyane Wade. The blend of teamwork, youth and experience was a wonderful combination, and allowed Miami to win the championship in 2006.

To round out his storied career, O'Neal would play with the Phoenix Suns, Cleveland Cavaliers and Boston Celtics. His numbers and contributions would decline in his final years, but everyone involved with those three teams loved having such a fun person on the team.

## Wilt Chamberlain

**Full Name:** Wilton Norman Chamberlain
**Nickname:** The Big Dipper
**Born:** August 21, 1936
**Hometown:** Philadelphia, Pennsylvania
**College:** Kansas
**Year Turned Pro:** 1959
**Total NBA Seasons:** 14
**Height:** 7'1"
**Position:** Center
**NBA Teams:** Philadelphia/San Francisco Warriors #13, Philadelphia 76ers #13, Los Angeles Lakers #13
**Notable Quote:**

---

*"I couldn't have come close without my teammates' help because the Knicks didn't want me to make 100."*

---

When you play a sports video game, you're usually allowed to increase or decrease the skills of players you create. For example, maybe in a basketball video game, the default shooting, passing, dribbling and jumping ability is 75. If you're having a little fun, you could toggle those numbers up to 95, to create a player who is essentially unstoppable. Feel free to thank me later for that idea!

The closest thing in real life we have ever seen to a video game-like character and player was Wilt Chamberlain. Some of the things he achieved on a basketball court feel like they are made up. Like the fact that he scored 100 points in a single game. Or that he averaged over 50 points a game for an entire season. Or that we actually don't really know how great he truly was, because the NBA did not keep track of blocks when Chamberlain played from 1959-1973.

That's the kind of legacy Chamberlain had in those days, and even after he retired. He was a larger-than-life figure who could do things that most other people couldn't.

Chamberlain loved to participate in track and field as a kid, running faster than the competition. However, he grew very tall very quickly! He was 6'11" in high school, which is pretty remarkable. Let's just say he didn't have to jump to reach the top of his door frames at home.

As you might imagine, there wasn't much other high school kids could do to stop Chamberlain on the basketball floor. He scored more than 2,200 points in three seasons as a high school basketball player, which is hard to believe. Rumor also has it that his teammates would miss shots on purpose, so that their towering center could take the ball and put it into the basket without much resistance.

This was also when Chamberlain earned himself a few different nicknames. It's important not to call people by names that make them feel bad, but Wilt enjoyed being called the Big Dipper. The name was in reference to a constellation of stars in the sky, but it also came about because the extremely tall student often had to dip his head to avoid hitting the ceiling.

The frenzy of attention around Chamberlain as he dominated the high school game was remarkable. Everyone across the country wondered where the teenager would decide to attend college. Since he was from Philadelphia, locals were hoping to continue to watch the massive player break all kinds of records in eastern Pennsylvania. Chamberlain would have a big decision to make, as he was recruited by over 200 universities across the United States.

But there was one college that seemed to want him the most. The University of Kansas would send prominent alumni to visit Chamberlain and talk with him about their experiences at the school. Head coach Phog Allen wanted the prospect to feel comfortable on campus, since he would be moving far away from where he'd grown up.

Chamberlain did end up becoming a Kansas Jayhawk, and is arguably the greatest player to ever play for the program. The competition was no match for the 7'1", 275-pound behemoth. In two phenomenal college seasons, Chamberlain would average nearly 30 points per game, and over 18 rebounds as well. He won the Most Outstanding Player award in 1957 for his efforts.

Before he joined the NBA, Chamberlain spent a year on the Harlem Globetrotters. They were (and still are) a team of players focused on making sure fans have fun at their games. The team does many fancy tricks with the basketball, and makes shots from great distances. Chamberlain's physical feats were a perfect match for the traveling roadshow.

There wasn't much doubt where Chamberlain would begin his NBA career. Back in those days, the league had something called a territorial draft, where teams could take players who grew up in their geographical area. The NBA did this so that hometown players could drive interest from fans who may have remembered them playing before they became professionals. This meant Chamberlain got to return home, because the Philadelphia Warriors selected him with the first pick.

Even though Chamberlain would go on to accomplish many things with the Warriors/76ers, as well as with the Los Angeles Lakers later in his career, he will always be remembered for what he did on March 2, 1962 in Hershey, Pennsylvania. The hoops legend would score a single-game record 100 points against the New York Knicks that night!

The gargantuan player would make 36 baskets for the game during the regular course of play, and he would make 28 free throws as well. Chamberlain was not known as a prolific free throw shooter, so the fact that he made 28 out of 32 attempts at the line was pretty remarkable.

One of the most iconic photos in basketball history was taken after that game, and it shows Wilt holding up a piece of paper with the number 100 written on it.

**Larry Bird**

**Full Name:** Larry Joe Bird
**Nickname:** Larry Legend
**Born:** December 7, 1956
**Hometown:** West Baden, Indiana
**College:** Indiana State
**Year Turned Pro:** 1979
**Total NBA Seasons:** 13
**Height:** 6'9"
**Position:** Small Forward
**NBA Team:** Boston Celtics #33
**Notable Quote:**

---

*"I have a theory that if you give 100% all of the time, somehow things will work out in the end."*

---

You may not realize it now, but you have many traits that you inherited from your parents. These can be anything from a physical feature, like when people tell you your eyes look like your mom's, to a personality quirk, like if you tell funny jokes just like your dad. It might even be something you don't want to admit to your friends in elementary or middle school because it's not cool to be like your parents... but one day that will probably change.

For NBA great Larry Bird, he and his mother might as well have been two peas in a pod. He watched her work very hard to earn just enough money to put food on the table for her six children. She was not easily rattled, and did not give up when things did not go her way. Larry himself would be known as someone who gave every bit of effort he could in life.

The two would end up needing to stick together, since his parents divorced when he was in high school and his father died when he was 18.

Through all of the trials and tests Bird faced as a boy, he was able to get away from it all doing one thing he loved more than anything: playing basketball. A hoop was hung on the back of a barn near where he grew up, and Bird would spend countless hours outside shooting there. It wasn't what someone in this day and age would call a proper court, but for Bird, it was a sanctuary where he could try everything that came into his mind.

The ability to feel comfortable taking any type of shot was something that Bird worked tirelessly to achieve. He would practice with both hands, and was sure to get a good amount of arc on his shots, to give the ball a chance to bounce in if his attempt wasn't perfect.

Even though he spent a lot of solo time improving his shot, Bird had a natural feel for how the game should be played. He was talented enough to take and make most shots, but understood the importance of getting his teammates involved. If the other players on the court had confidence and played well, that would only help give Bird better opportunities at a shot.

This unselfishness and team-oriented attitude was on full display during Bird's college career at nearby Indiana State. While averaging over 30 points per game, the savvy forward was still able to put up over four assists and more than two steals per contest. The numbers and the highlights showed that Bird would do anything it took for his team to win the game.

During the 1978-1979 college basketball season, the Indiana State Sycamores did a lot of winning. In fact, they won every single game leading up to the national championship. The Sycamores would play the Michigan State Spartans, led by Magic Johnson, in the title game. While Indiana State fell short of finishing off a perfect campaign, a historic basketball rivalry would start that night between Bird and Magic Johnson.

The Boston Celtics had their eyes on Bird for a couple of years, as they hoped to rebuild their roster with a young player that could take the NBA by storm. He would do just that from day one, as Bird won the league's Rookie of the Year award, and also helped Boston increase their win total immensely.

It would be the beginning of a great run for the Celtics, who would go on to win three NBA championships in the 1980's thanks to Bird's masterful play. In an era that featured many other future Hall of Famers, Bird stood out as one of the very best, capturing three Most Valuable Player awards in the decade as well.

The 6'9" forward could do anything the team asked of him. Bird could match up with other forwards on the perimeter defensively, while also crashing the glass and serving as a de facto point guard. He was fearless, and loved a challenge. One of the best examples of this was his duel with Dominique Wilkins of the Atlanta Hawks in the 1988 playoffs. Wilkins poured in 47 points in a win or go home Game 7, but Bird scored 20 points in the fourth quarter to secure the victory.

Bird also has one of the coolest distinctions in league history. The NBA introduced a three-point shooting competition as part of their All-Star weekend festivities in 1985, and the Celtics' sharpshooter won the event in each of its first three years. It helped kick off what would eventually become a three-point revolution in the game, so it's only fitting that one of the best marksmen in history started it off on a good note.

In the last couple years of his career, Bird struggled to remain healthy, but would finish his playing days strong. He was named to the 1992 United States Olympic basketball 'Dream Team,' where he would play with two other GOATs, Michael Jordan and Magic Johnson. The last game Bird ever played was the gold medal matchup with Croatia, which added another accomplishment to the Indiana native's resume.

**Baby Goats**

There are some who might think that other names should have cracked my GOAT top 10 rankings. While I feel pretty good about my list, here are five other players who deserve to be mentioned, and who fell just short of the top 10.

**Bill Russell**

Put simply, Bill Russell is the NBA's ultimate winner. There is a great picture of the former Celtics legend holding all 11 of his championship rings, with a wide smile plastered across his face. No player in the history of the sport can claim that many titles.

Even though Russell could score, he made his greatest impact on the defensive end of the floor. As his notable quote suggests, he wanted offensive players to feel like they were going to get their shot blocked any time he was in the area. Jumping in the air with his hands held high on every possession is how he made his presence felt.

## Hakeem Olajuwon

Even though he was seven feet tall, you would have a difficult time finding anyone who was more coordinated than Hakeem Olajuwon. His athleticism allowed him to move around slower centers, and he could trick other players with a bunch of fakes that left him with open shots.

Olajuwon was a master at using his feet in order to make the defensive player uncomfortable, to get himself into a position to lay the ball into the basket. He was the main reason the Rockets won two consecutive championships in 1994 and 1995, but Olajuwon always shared credit with his teammates.

## Oscar Robertson

In basketball statistics, one of the most impressive accomplishments is a triple double. While it's a funny name, it's pretty easy to understand. A triple double is when a player gets 10 or more of something in three different basketball categories. For example, if someone scores 15 points, makes 13 assists, and grabs 10 rebounds, they've accomplished a triple double.

For many decades, there was no player who was more associated with a triple double than Oscar Robertson. In order to do that once, let alone 181 times, which Robertson did, you have to be a player who is good at multiple things on the basketball court. Robertson certainly was, and his numbers proved it.

## Kevin Durant

At every level of basketball, there are certain players who just seem to be able to score points easier than others. Whether it's a fellow youth player with a smooth jump shot, or an adult who makes athletic layups at the basket, some players just get buckets no matter what!

Kevin Durant absolutely falls into that group. There isn't a lot a defender can do to stop him, so the best they can hope is that he will take a difficult shot. Durant is so skilled that he can make those tough attempts even far away from the basket, and it feels like he has a move for every type of game situation.

## Jerry West

Take a good look at the NBA logo. It seems like the player is about to drive the ball to the basket with his left hand, ready to go up for a shot or maybe set up a teammate for an easy shot. It's one of the perfect images to associate with the game of basketball.

But that silhouette wasn't just randomly picked. It was actually modeled after a real picture of Jerry West. He was one of the sport's greatest players in its early years, and was known for making baskets at the end of games.

One of the most famous shots he ever made came in the 1970 NBA Finals, when he made a basket from beyond halfcourt to send the game into overtime!

# 4

# AMAZING GAMES

As I'm sure you already know, basketball can be so much fun! There are many different ways players can contribute to a game, and the excitement of getting together to play is truly special.

Whether you've played in hundreds of games, or only a few so far, I have no doubt that there are certain games that stick out in your mind more than others, for different reasons. Maybe you were playing at the hoop in your schoolyard during lunchtime and someone made a game-winning basket just as the period was about to end. Perhaps your buddy made a crazy reverse layup that surprised everyone on the floor. Maybe it's a defensive performance that is memorable, where you helped slow down a really talented player.

Even at the highest level of the sport, there are a handful of special games that come to mind faster than the rest. I've compiled a list of some of the most amazing games in NBA history, which unfolded with about as much drama as some of the best books you've read in school.

I'll explain who the main players were, and why the game was so important in NBA history. Get ready to feel like you were a part of the action as we go through some outstanding performances and endings.

I encourage you to use your imagination to picture how the games played out as I describe them, and then go ahead and pull up highlights of these games later. You won't be disappointed.

## 2002 WESTERN CONFERENCE FINALS (WCF) GAME 4: SACRAMENTO KINGS AT LOS ANGELES LAKERS

In the early 2000's, the Los Angeles Lakers were an unstoppable freight train that no one could seem to stop. They had won back-to-back NBA championships in the 2000 and 2001 seasons, and there didn't seem to be any strong challengers who could knock them off the throne.

Enter the 2002 Sacramento Kings, who did not quite have the star power of the Lakers, but played team basketball. Each player happily passed the ball to their teammates, and willingly moved without the ball to find open shots. Their unselfishness made them very difficult to guard, and they had a fantastic regular season that year.

Led by Kobe Bryant and Shaquille O'Neal, however, Los Angeles just seemed to be too powerful for Sacramento to beat. The two teams would face one another in the 2002 Western Conference Finals, and the winner would go to the NBA Finals that year. Whichever team won four games first out of a possible seven would win the series.

It became pretty clear early on in the Western Conference Finals that the Kings were going to give the Lakers a lot of trouble. Their style was unique, and Los Angeles had not really faced a team like them, whose ball movement was so sharp.

The Kings would win two out of the first three games, setting up a massively important Game 4 in Los Angeles. If Sacramento won, there would be a very good chance that the Lakers dynasty would be over. If Los Angeles was victorious, they would reclaim momentum on their way to a third straight title.

The game started brilliantly for Sacramento, and disastrously for Los Angeles. In the first half, it felt like the Kings made every open jump shot, while the Lakers struggled to get their offense going. Things appeared to come easily for Sacramento, while every attempt to score for Los Angeles seemed hard.

Now, even though it didn't seem too important at the time, Lakers forward Samaki Walker made a shot from halfcourt at the buzzer at the end of the first half. Los Angeles was still losing, but this raised the spirits of the players and their fans. Fans watching on TV noticed that Walker actually did not release the ball before the buzzer sounded… so the points shouldn't have counted, but back then, referees could not check the replay, so the three crucial points remained on the board.

(Today, of course, referees can double check to see if a shot was released before the clock ran out.)

When the players returned to the court for the second half, the score got extremely close. The Lakers' defense tightened up, and they were able to find a rhythm on offense. The game would come down to the last few seconds of the fourth quarter.

With under 10 seconds to go in the game, Sacramento had a 99-97 lead. Los Angeles had the ball, looking to extend the game into overtime, or even win it. Bryant drove to the basket, and flipped up a shot that went off the rim. O'Neal caught the rebound, but his shot was short and came off the rim hard.

At that precise moment, it seemed like the Lakers dynasty might be over. Sacramento would take a 3-1 lead in the series, and a new team would represent the Western Conference in the NBA Finals.

Except... something crazy happened.

Kings center Vlade Divac tipped the ball back towards the three-point line after O'Neal missed the putback shot. He did this trying to waste time and keep the ball away from the Lakers' stars.

There was only one problem - the ball bounced right to Los Angeles forward Robert Horry, who was standing behind the three-point line. With supreme confidence, Horry took the shot, and the ball went in at the buzzer. The Lakers won!

The crowd went absolutely bonkers, and the series was even at two games apiece. Los Angeles would go on to win the series, and then the championship. But they wouldn't have gotten there if not for the amazing shot by Horry.

## 2007 EASTERN CONFERENCE FINALS GAME 5: CLEVELAND CAVALIERS AT DETROIT PISTONS

For several years, the story surrounding Cleveland Cavaliers star LeBron James was that he was different. He was the most special prospect to come into the league in a long time, and greatness was expected from him from the first day he played in the NBA.

James displayed his remarkable talent literally from his first game, and was showing that he could affect a game in many different ways. His tremendous athleticism allowed him to finish plays with thunderous dunks that revved up the crowd. James was also an incredible passer, finding his teammates cutting to the basket or spotting up for open three-point shots.

Of course, he was also able to put the ball in the basket himself, averaging 20 points as a rookie and then 27 as a second-year player.

His sensational talent did help the Cavaliers win more games each year, but it wasn't translating into enough victories to be serious playoff contenders.

However, that would all change in the 2007 season, as James and the Cavaliers would make a surprising run to the Eastern Conference Finals against the Detroit

Pistons. Detroit would be a really tough opponent for Cleveland, because of Detroit's historic ability to play excellent defense and stop teams from scoring.

Detroit clamped down on the Cavaliers in the first two games of the series, beating Cleveland in both matchups while limiting them to just 76 points in each game. But Cleveland was able to make some changes that helped them score more points in Games 3 and 4, and they were able to beat Detroit in those games, which surprised many.

With the series tied at two games each, the winner of the crucial Game 5 would have an excellent chance to advance. The fifth game was in Detroit, so Pistons fans would be thunderously loud and try to distract the Cavaliers.

The game was close throughout, and was tied at 70 when it entered the fourth quarter. It seemed like Detroit's tough starting five would wear down Cleveland, but James put his team on his back.

Game 5 would remain tied after the fourth quarter, and after the first overtime as well! It went into a second overtime, and the Cavaliers eventually won when James scored a layup with 0.2 seconds remaining.

That's how it ended, but you may be wondering how the Cavs got there. During the final period and overtime, James was spectacular. He made difficult jump shots, determined drives to the basket, and threw down some ferocious dunks. The funny thing was, the Pistons knew exactly who the ball would go to on every possession, but they couldn't stop him.

At one point in the fourth quarter and then during the two overtimes, James scored 25 straight points for the Cavaliers, without anyone else on his team scoring during that stretch. It's safe to say that this game proved that the emerging superstar would be as great a player as everyone expected him to be.

The Cavaliers would win that series, making the NBA Finals, but lost the championship to the San Antonio Spurs.

### 1995 NBA FINALS GAME 1: HOUSTON ROCKETS AT ORLANDO MAGIC

Michael Jordan missed the entire 1994 NBA season and most of the 1995 season when he decided to take a break from basketball to play professional baseball. The rest of the league's eyes lit up during this time.

Other teams would now have a chance to win a title!

The Houston Rockets took full advantage of His Airness' absence in 1994, putting together a strong team that defeated the New York Knicks in the NBA Finals that year. The roster was built around superstar center Hakeem Olajuwon, who was one of the most skilled players in the league at that time.

In 1995, the Rockets had an uneven performance during the regular season, and it didn't seem like they were a strong bet to defend the title. But they squeaked into the Western Conference playoffs that year.

Meanwhile, the young, hungry, athletic Orlando Magic team dominated its way through the Eastern Conference. Led by youthful stars Shaquille O'Neal and Penny Hardaway, the Magic cast a spell on the rest of the league.

While the veteran Rockets were able to use their intelligence and experience to return to the Finals in 1995, the Magic used the enthusiasm of their fresh-faced stars to get to the title series.

It was such an interesting matchup, because O'Neal and Olajuwon would go head-to-head, but they had different styles. Game 1 would set the tone.

Orlando came out on fire, outscoring Houston 30-19 in the first quarter. It seemed like the Rockets' veterans were a step slow early on.

But sure enough, the defending champs would bounce back. They took over the game in the third quarter, scoring 37 points to Orlando's 19 in that period. This meant Game 1 would come down to the fourth quarter.

With a few seconds remaining, the Magic were clinging for dear life to a three-point lead. The Rockets had to foul Orlando in order to extend the game, so they fouled Magic forward Nick Anderson.

At that point, Anderson had scored 22 points, and was playing very well. If he could make some free throws, the chances that the Rockets could come back would significantly decrease.

Anderson stepped to the line and missed his first attempt. It wasn't a big deal. If he made the second shot, Orlando would have a four-point lead.

But he missed the second shot too! There was a scramble for the rebound, and the ball ended up back in Anderson's hands, who was fouled once more. Second chances don't always present themselves during games, but Anderson had a chance to make up for his earlier misses.

Unbelievably, Anderson missed two more free throws, and the Rockets came down with the next possession and made a game-tying three-pointer to send the game to overtime!

In the extra period, Houston's experience proved to be the difference, and they won Game 1. They would also be victorious in Games 2, 3, and 4, so were on their way to a second consecutive title.

The Rockets' determination cannot be ignored, but it is also important to point out how the Magic responded to Anderson's missed free throws in the first game. They did not blame their loss on their teammate, or make him feel worse when he was already upset.

Orlando players said that if they had made a couple more plays earlier in Game 1, it would not have come down to those free throws at the end. That is an example of a team sticking together no matter what happens.

## 1997 NBA FINALS GAME 5: CHICAGO BULLS AT UTAH JAZZ

The combined scores of the first four games of the 1997 NBA Finals were separated by a total of two points. Not surprisingly, the Chicago Bulls and Utah Jazz each won two games, and the winner of the championship would need to take two out of the next three games to bring home the trophy.

The math was simple enough, but there was only one problem for the Bulls. Michael Jordan was sick heading into Game 5.

There have been a lot of different stories about this illness over the years. One version involves Jordan getting hungry late in the evening the night before Game 5. There weren't any restaurants open when the Bulls star wanted a bite to eat, so his options were limited. Someone located a pizza place in Utah that was still open and would deliver a pie to Jordan's hotel.

The pizza showed up at Jordan's door, and he devoured it. Now he could go to bed feeling full and wake up fresh and ready to go the next morning. Except that didn't happen. Jordan's stomach went topsy turvy in the middle of the night, and he couldn't get to sleep. He was also weak.

And that's the legendary pizza-gate tale!

Another version of the story involves Jordan having the flu. You know those days when you have a headache, fever and your nose is stuffed up? Maybe your parents keep you home from school and make you stay in bed, bringing you soup and ginger ale.

Jordan could have stayed in bed and missed Game 5, but he was determined to play. But he did not look like himself, and was already very sweaty at the beginning of the game. He did not run up and down the court with the same energy he usually had.

One thing he did on the bench during that game, which so many of us do when we are sick, was drink a lot of fluids. This helps an illness pass through your body more quickly, which is what Jordan hoped would help him feel better.

Despite everything that was tried to make him feel better, it was still a struggle. Jordan was even seen leaning on Scottie Pippen's shoulder, as Scottie tried to help him through the game. Shockingly, number 23 somehow played 44 out of a possible 48 minutes in the game.

The amazing thing about the "Flu Game" was that Jordan played better than most players who were healthy! He scored a game high 38 points, and the Bulls needed every single one. Chicago ended up winning the game by a final score of 90-88.

It was one of the most inspirational performances in NBA history, as perhaps the greatest player of all-time continued to display greatness when he should have been sick in bed.

Chicago would go on to win Game 6 as well, and capture their fifth championship of that decade.

## 2016 NBA FINALS GAME 7: CLEVELAND CAVALIERS AT GOLDEN STATE WARRIORS

The weight of a tortured basketball fanbase versus the prospect of being crowned as the greatest team of all time. Sounds like a big-time showdown, doesn't it?

That's precisely what was at stake during the 2016 NBA Finals, which featured the Cleveland Cavaliers taking on the Golden State Warriors.

The Cavaliers were a franchise that had approached the mountaintop on several occasions throughout their history, but could never quite get over the top. Though there were some solid Cleveland teams led by head coach Mike Fratello in the 1980's and 1990's, and one that made a surprise run to the NBA Finals in 2007 but lost, things never broke right for the Cavs when it mattered most.

Adding insult to injury was the departure of favored Ohio son LeBron James during the summer of 2010. In a highly public free agent courting, James was wooed by other teams to sign a contract to leave Cleveland, and he ended up going to the Miami Heat. The Cavaliers' chances to contend for a title walked right out the door with James.

But after his four seasons with the Heat, James decided to return to his first NBA home. In 2015, he led the Cavaliers back to the NBA Finals, though they lost in six games to the Warriors.

Now let's flip our attention for a moment over to Golden State's story. Their 2015-2016 regular season was incredible. It started off with one of the longest winning streaks in NBA history. The Warriors won their first 24 games to start off the campaign. They continued to breeze through their schedule, dropping only four games before the All-Star break in the middle of the year.

It was clear early on that they were going to clinch homecourt advantage throughout the playoffs, so they had to decide whether they wanted to set the regular season wins record, or rest their players ahead of a long playoff run. Golden State decided to try to set the mark, and maintained their wonderful winning ways. The Warriors won their 73rd game, the final game of the regular season, which was the most wins in any single season in league history.

The anticipation, buildup and excitement of this matchup culminated in a historic Game 7 of the NBA Finals. A lot was at stake, and you could feel the intensity through your TV screen.

As things grew tense, shots were missed, and the two teams combined for the lowest point total in Game 7 than in any other game of the series. Both teams upped the pressure defensively, as the Cavaliers' taller players tried to keep Warriors guard Steph Curry covered in pick and roll situations.

For four straight minutes near the end of the fourth quarter, neither team could make a hoop! Someone was going to have to do something extraordinary to secure the championship for their team.

Then, with less than two minutes left, it seemed like the Warriors were going to score easily on a fast break layup by Andre Iguodala. As Iguodala was going up to score, James sprinted back on defense and swooped in for a legendary chase down block, which denied Golden State the easy basket. It was an enormous play that swung the momentum back in Cleveland's direction.

On the other end, the Cavaliers had a chance to take the lead for good. What type of play would they run for such an important possession? Somewhat surprisingly, the ball was given to Kyrie Irving, who would try to get a good shot up over Curry. After a few dribbles, Irving pulled up for three, and nailed the basket!

Golden State was not able to answer, and the Cavaliers were NBA champions for the first time in their history!

## 1970 NBA FINALS GAME 7: LOS ANGELES LAKERS AT NEW YORK KNICKS

In the early days of the NBA, there were a few franchises that were the gold standard of the league. For the first two or three decades, many of the original teams in the biggest cities had the most attention paid to them.

When the Los Angeles Lakers and New York Knicks met in the 1970 NBA Finals, fans on both coasts were pumped. You had the concrete jungle that is New York City, compared with the glitz and glamour of Los Angeles. It was like a script for an edge-of-your-seat action movie!

Of course, a film is only as good as the actors involved in the production, and this one had some pretty big stars. You had Wilt Chamberlain playing center for Los Angeles, who was still putting up astronomical statistics. Jerry West was a humble star, but he was one of the NBA's best clutch players at that time.

New York had a sensational backcourt, led by Walt "Clyde" Frazier and Earl "The Pearl" Monroe. The

Knicks also had a great center in Willis Reed, who would need to do battle with Chamberlain if they had any hope of winning the title.

While there were several amazing games to choose from in this series, including nailbiters in Games 2 and 3, we're going to lock in on a Game 7 that would decide whether the championship was headed to the East Coast or the West Coast.

Through the first four games, Reed had more than stood up to the task of performing against Chamberlain. He played exceptionally, including a 38-point, 17-rebound masterpiece in a Game 3 victory.

It seemed like the two big men would duke it out for the remainder of the series, but the plot changed dramatically in Game 5. Reed would tear a muscle in his thigh (yikes!) during that contest, and was only able to play eight minutes. While the Knicks were able to hold on to win that game, they lost to the Lakers in Game 6.

New York's spirits were a little down heading into Game 7, because it looked like they weren't going to be at full strength for the ultimate game. Reed was injured, and it didn't seem like the Knicks would have enough to fend off the mighty Lakers.

Remember how we set this up as a movie? What does any good flick have?

A shocking ending!

During pregame warmups, Reed hobbled on to the court to shoot around with his teammates. But no one ever thought he would be able to suit up. Reed later said that this was going to be his best chance to win a title, and he did not want to look back and regret not trying to play.

Somehow, some way, Reed was able to play 27 minutes in Game 7. He made two iconic baskets to begin the game. Although he would not score again, those shots gave the Knicks a huge emotional lift at the most pivotal point of their season. It was a gutty effort that would be remembered throughout NBA history.

Add to that the fact that Clyde Frazier had arguably the best game of his career that night, recording 36 points, 19 assists and seven rebounds. The Knicks would go on to win the NBA title, their first in franchise history.

## 1965 EASTERN CONFERENCE FINALS GAME 7: PHILADELPHIA 76ERS AT BOSTON CELTICS

There are very few teams in sports history who are identified by their team name and a decade. The 1920's

New York Yankees. The 1980's Edmonton Oilers. The 1970's Pittsburgh Steelers. Fans just know the type of excellence demonstrated by these franchises over that memorable period of time.

Right at the top of the list are the 1960's Boston Celtics, who were a juggernaut during that decade. They won a remarkable 11 titles in a 13-year stretch from 1957 through 1969. Legendary head coach Red Auerbach was known for celebrating on the bench when it was clear that Boston would take home the victory. The Celtics were truly the first NBA dynasty.

While their roster was stacked with future basketball Hall of Famers, their approach to each game involved doing whatever it took to win. It didn't matter who scored the most points, who made the game-winning shot, or who got the most attention. If the team brought home the championship, everyone would be able to bask in the glory of being the best.

When you've finished your homework and completed your chores, take a look at some of the scoring averages for Boston's players during that time. You may notice that a lot of their opponents have one or two players getting most of the baskets, but with the Celtics, it's pretty evenly distributed across multiple players.

For example, in the 1964-1965 season, six players averaged 10 or more points per game. This means that players bought into the idea of passing the ball to the player with the open shot on most possessions.

During that season, Boston was looking to win its seventh straight championship, but as you might imagine, other teams in the league were getting a little tired of the Celtics' dominance. One of those teams was the Philadelphia 76ers, who had fallen to Boston in the playoffs for several years prior.

Wilt Chamberlain was on the roster at the time, and was casually averaging 30 points and 22 rebounds per game—no big deal. The 76ers were centered (pun intended) around their center, and everyone else kind of fit in around him.

As it turned out, the 76ers and Celtics would cross paths again in the 1965 playoffs, and their Eastern Conference Finals playoff series would be one for the ages. Each team alternated wins for the first six games of the series, setting the stage for a monumental Game 7. Boston's dynastic run was in serious jeopardy, and it would take a strong effort to keep the streak alive.

The game was close throughout, as the stars came to play in this critical matchup. Chamberlain played incredibly, while Bill Russell and Sam Jones also laid down remarkable performances. The right to represent the Eastern Conference in the NBA Finals came down to the final seconds.

It seemed like Boston had things wrapped up. They were up by one point, and had the ball. One of the Celtics players was likely to be fouled, and to put the game away with two free throws (there was no three-point shot at this time). All they had to do was inbound the ball.

That proved to be a challenge. Russell tried to pass to a teammate, but the basketball struck a wire that was linked near the backboard. The ball fell back out of bounds, and Philadelphia found themselves with one opportunity to win the game.

All they had to do was inbound the ball...

Philadelphia's Hal Greer tried to pass it to a teammate, but Celtics forward John Havlicek stole the ball, in one of the most iconic plays in NBA playoff history.

The play is made even more electric by the call of Celtics radio play by play announcer Johnny Most, who loses his mind when it happens. "Havlicek stole the ball!" has actually been its own exhibit at the Basketball Hall of Fame in Massachusetts.

Boston's streak of excellence would continue thanks to Havlicek's cat-like quickness as the most important point of the season.

## 2013 NBA FINALS GAME 6: SAN ANTONIO SPURS AT MIAMI HEAT

Do you know what a heat index is? Usually, it has to do with the weather in the summertime, and is a number used to explain how hot it actually feels outside.

Basketball fans think of the Heat Index (yes, in capital letters) as something else. It was created to watch every move of what many call the first super team in NBA history. In the summer of 2010, star free agents Chris Bosh and LeBron James would join Dwyane Wade on the Miami Heat. Everyone was extremely curious to find out how successful a franchise with that much talent was going to do. Would they all be willing to sacrifice for the greater good of the team?

When the Heat introduced Wade, James and Bosh together for the first time, they openly wondered how many championships they would win.

Before the 2012-2013 season, the answer to that question was one. Miami had fallen in the NBA Finals in 2011 to the veteran-laden Dallas Mavericks. But in

2012, the Heat would prevail over the talented but youthful Oklahoma City Thunder.

The Heat would continue to march through the competition during the regular season and postseason, qualifying for a third straight NBA Finals in 2013, this time against the San Antonio Spurs. This would be a much tougher test than the previous two title series, since the Spurs had athleticism, experience and chemistry from many years of playing together.

San Antonio's Tim Duncan, Manu Ginobili and Tony Parker had won three titles together, and were searching for their first championship since 2007. Forward Kawhi Leonard was an emerging star, thanks to his relentless toughness and the physical defensive pressure he could put on the opposing team's best players.

This blueprint created a lot of trouble for Miami, who found themselves down three games to two heading into a must-win situation in Game 6.

San Antonio had been through high profile close-out games before, and would not make mistakes that would give Miami easy opportunities. The Spurs had a 10-point lead in the fourth quarter, and were positioned to finish off their opponent.

The Heat were down three points with 20 seconds left in the fourth quarter. They could decide to go for a quick two points, and then foul the Spurs to extend the game, or they could go for a three-pointer to try and tie things up.

Miami would choose the second option, and ran a play to get James a wide open look at a three pointer. The ball bounced off the rim, and it seemed like the Heat were going to lose in devastating fashion.

But that's not what happened. Bosh jumped high for the rebound, and secured the ball. There was now less than 10 seconds left in the fourth quarter, and he had to think fast. So did every one of his teammates, including Ray Allen.

By that point, Allen was nearing the end of his amazing NBA career, and was on the Heat in order to space the floor with his pinpoint shooting ability. In his younger days, he'd been a star, and plays would be designed to get him chances to score. With Miami, Allen's role was to roam around the perimeter and knock down open shots to keep defenses honest.

Allen had taken thousands of three-point shots in his life, and knew he had to act quickly while Bosh gathered himself. He back-peddled to a spot behind the three-point line in the corner of the court. Bosh looked up and passed him the ball.

With Parker closing in on him quickly, Allen rose up and drilled a three pointer to tie the game!

It would eventually go into overtime, and Miami was able to hold on to force a Game 7.

Game 7 was a defensive struggle, but the Heat would prevail over the Spurs and win their second title in three years. None of it would've been possible had it not been for Allen's heroics.

## 2006 REGULAR SEASON: TORONTO RAPTORS AT LOS ANGELES LAKERS

I hope you've learned many cool facts in this book that you can share with your friends and family. One of those little nuggets was that the record for most points scored in a single game by a player is held by Wilt Chamberlain, who scored 100 points against the New York Knicks in 1962.

Here's one of the most fun debates to have about basketball. Do you think it's possible for anyone to ever break that record? It would take someone getting video-game level hot with their shooting, and it might also involve teammates consistently passing a player the ball to help him get the record.

Needless to say, a lot of things would have to go right for anyone to even come close to challenging Chamberlain's mark.

But on one Sunday night, while many NBA fans were already tucked into their beds, a player actually did come close to that seemingly unreachable number.

Los Angeles Lakers legend Kobe Bryant would have a banner night on January 22, 2006 against the Toronto Raptors. His ankle was a little bit sore, but he gave it a go during a game that he felt the Lakers needed to win.

The game began with Bryant displaying his usual scoring greatness. He would make it to the basket several times and finish through contact. Bryant connected on jump shot after jump shot, as if a magnet was pulling the ball through the hoop. His ability to put points on the board was dazzling, and he ended the first half with a total of 26.

That's a really impressive half for any player, but it isn't anything that fans haven't seen before. Perhaps most important for Bryant personally was the fact that even though he was having a good night in the scoring column, his team was losing to Toronto by a large margin.

The Raptors were able to keep their foot on the gas and maintain a sizeable lead in the third quarter. With none of his teammates really shooting well that night, the onus remained on Kobe to keep his team in the game.

He did just that. It's not like the Raptors didn't know Bryant would be the focal point of the offense, but there wasn't much they could do to stop him. Bryant would make pull up three-pointers, difficult fadeaways, and pick-off passes that led to easy dunks on the other end of the floor.

The onslaught became too much for the Raptors to deal with. The significant lead that they had built up was completely erased, thanks to Bryant. Once the Lakers took the lead, they still needed Bryant to maintain his momentum to keep Toronto at bay.

The game script was perfect for Bryant to stay in aggressive point-seeking mode, because had the game been decided earlier, he likely would've been benched.

The crowd chanted Kobe's name throughout his 55-point second half barrage, and as he kept adding to his total at the free throw line.

While it is often said in sports that moments are groundbreaking or unique, this is one that will truly withstand the test of time, when Kobe Bryant made 81 points in a single game.

## 1993 WESTERN CONFERENCE SEMIFINALS GAME 6: PHOENIX SUNS AT SAN ANTONIO SPURS

NBC sports play-by-play commentator Dick Enberg put it best during the 1993 NBA Playoffs, when he said that Charles Barkley was having the year of a basketball lifetime.

Barkley hit the jackpot in so many different ways.

He'd started his career with the Philadelphia 76ers, as a young player learning from NBA legends like Julius Erving and Maurice Cheeks. However, as they got older and aged out of the league, the 76ers started to become less competitive, even though Barkley had developed into a clear-cut All-Star. He was in the prime of his career with the 76ers in the early 1990's, but his best years were being used up on a team that struggled to remain relevant.

In the summer of 1992, Barkley's NBA prospects would change dramatically. He was traded for three players to the Phoenix Suns, a team who was in the hunt to make the NBA Finals every year.

That wasn't all that was going right for Barkley. He was also named to the 1992 Olympic Team, which is more famously known in basketball history as The Dream

Team. The collection of basketball greats would have a fun time hanging out on and off the court in Barcelona, Spain. Barkley got to see a different part of the world, and dominate the competition en route to winning a gold medal.

When he returned home for the NBA season, Barkley was motivated to remind people just how great he could be. In his first year with the Suns, Barkley was a man on a mission, along with the rest of his teammates. They finished with the best regular season record in the league, and had legitimate hopes of making the NBA Finals.

However, the Western Conference was loaded that year, and one obstacle in the Suns' way were the San Antonio Spurs. They were led by center David Robinson, whose physical gifts were as amazing as any player in the league. He could run the floor like a guard, had the athleticism of a dynamic small forward, but was also 7'1".

The two Dream Team teammates and All-Stars would square off in a memorable second round series in the 1993 NBA Playoffs. Both Robinson and Barkley would play phenomenally, carrying their teams for the first five games of the series. Phoenix held a 3-2 lead heading into a crucial Game 6.

At home, the Spurs seemed to be poised to force a Game 7. Robinson was excellent on both ends of the floor, and San Antonio got balanced scoring from the likes of Sean Elliot and Dale Ellis. The Suns were going to need to find an answer quickly if they wanted to end the series right there and then.

Phoenix made a great comeback, and evened up the score at 100 each. With 10 seconds left in regulation, the Suns would have a chance to officially continue their season in the Western Conference Finals.

Suns coach Paul Westphal put the ball in the hands of his best player. Barkley looked up at the clock, and then looked straight ahead to find the large Robinson hoping to shut him down.

Barkley milked the clock, wanting his final attempt at the hoop to be the last shot of the fourth quarter. He took a couple of dribbles towards Robinson, then quickly stepped back. The Spurs center was not as close to challenging Barkley's attempt as he would've hoped, and Barkley drilled the long two-pointer to give the Suns the win!

It was a great moment in NBA history because of the excitement of the finish, and because one player achieved their goal with another great directly in his way. To be the best, you have to beat the best, and Barkley did that on that night.

# 5

# INCREDIBLE FACTS

There's no doubt that watching YouTube videos in the cafeteria and trying to find out which of your friends has the most delicious snack at lunch is a good time. It's always great to catch up with your buddies and laugh hysterically over the newest inside joke.

So while you've got your phones out (let's be honest, when are they not out!?), you might want to DM your friends about a bunch of amazing NBA facts I've included below. They're mostly about memorable performances, funny moments, great teams and notable people throughout the history of the game.

I hope you enjoy reading about this as much as I enjoyed putting them together for you!

**100.** Danny Biasone invented the 24-second shot clock in 1954, which meant teams could no longer hold the ball for several minutes.

**99.** Dallas Mavericks guard Bubba Wells once fouled out of an NBA game in three minutes.

**98.** The highest scoring game in NBA history was between the Detroit Pistons and Denver Nuggets in 1983. The Pistons won 186-184.

**97.** Seattle SuperSonics guard Dale Ellis once played 69 minutes in an NBA game. That's the most in league history.

**96.** Philadelphia Warriors center Wilt Chamberlain grabbed the most rebounds ever in an NBA game, with 55.

**95.** Orlando Magic point guard Scott Skiles made the most assists ever in an NBA game, with 30.

**94.** The Los Angeles Lakers franchise originated in Minneapolis, which has a lot of lakes surrounding the city. When the team moved to the West Coast, they kept the name.

**93.** The first three-point line in the NBA came in 1979. Before that, all shots from the court were worth two points or one point for a free throw.

**92.** Only four players have ever recorded a quadruple-double (10 or more of something in four different categories). They are Nate Thurmond, Alvin Robertson, Hakeem Olajuwon and David Robinson.

**91.** The Boston Celtics and Los Angeles Lakers have each won 17 championships, tied for the most of any team in NBA history.

**90.** Spalding was the official game ball partner of the NBA from 1983-2021. Today, Wilson provides the basketballs for NBA games.

**89.** Violet Palmer became the first female official to work an NBA game on October 30, 1997.

**88.** Toronto Raptors guard Jose Calderon set the record for free throw percentage in a season in 2008-2009. He made 98 percent of his attempts from the free throw line that year.

**87.** Minnesota Timberwolves guard Michael Williams made the most consecutive free throws in a row, with 97.

**86.** Golden State Warriors guard Klay Thompson scored 37 points in a quarter in 2015, which is the most points in any quarter in NBA history.

**85.** A.C. Green played in 1,192 consecutive NBA games, the longest streak in history.

**84.** The longest winning streak in NBA history belongs to the Los Angeles Lakers, who won 33 straight games in the 1971-1972 season.

**83.** The Larry O'Brien trophy is given to the team that wins the NBA title. It is over 25 inches tall, and weighs about 30 pounds.

**82.** The NBA schedule has consisted of 82 regular season games since the 1967-1968 season.

**81.** Utah Jazz point guard John Stockton has the most career assists and steals in NBA history.

**80.** The shortest player to ever play in an NBA game was Muggsy Bogues, who was 5'3".

**79.** The tallest players to ever play in an NBA game were Manute Bol and Gheorghe Muresan, who both stood at 7'7".

**78.** Phoenix Suns center Oliver Miller was the heaviest player to ever play in an NBA game, clocking in at 375 pounds.

**77.** The longest game in NBA history was six overtimes, played by the Indianapolis Olympians and Rochester Royals in 1951.

**76.** In the 2011 Slam Dunk Contest, Los Angeles Clippers forward Blake Griffin jumped over a car.

**75.** Richard Bavetta refereed 2,635 NBA games, the most of any official ever.

**74.** Boston Celtics shooting guard Chris Ford made the first three-point shot in NBA history in 1979.

**73.** 45-year-old Nat Hickey was the oldest player to play in an NBA game.

**72.** 18-year-old Andrew Bynum was the youngest player to play in an NBA game.

**71.** Dirk Nowitzki (Germany) scored the most career points of any non-American-born player.

**70.** Utah Jazz power forward Karl Malone has made the most career free throws, with 9,787.

**69.** The 1981-1982 Denver Nuggets averaged the most points per game for a team in a season, with 126.5.

**68.** Larry Brown is the only coach to win a college Division One championship and an NBA championship.

**67.** 430 players born in California have played in the NBA, the most of any state.

**66.** Canada has produced the most NBA players of any non-U.S. country, with 36.

**65.** Only one player ever born in New Hampshire made the NBA, and that was forward Matt Bonner.

**64.** Broadcaster Mike Breen has called more NBA Finals games on TV than anyone else.

**63.** Golden State Warriors forward Rick Barry used to shoot his free throws underhanded.

**62.** The NBA Finals MVP trophy is named after Bill Russell.

**61.** There are 11 NBA teams that have never won a championship. They are the Pacers, Hornets, Nets, Grizzlies, Jazz, Suns, Pelicans, Clippers, Nuggets, Magic and Timberwolves.

**60.** Jason Kidd and John Drew each had a game where they turned the ball over 14 times, which is an NBA record.

**59.** The New York Knicks have played the most games on Christmas than any team in NBA history.

**58.** The NBA has not scheduled a game on Thanksgiving since 2010.

**57.** Vince Carter is the only player to appear in an NBA game in four different decades.

**56.** The first game located outside of the U.S. took place in Israel in 1978 between the Washington Bullets and Maccabi Tel Aviv.

**55.** The most points ever scored in the first game of an NBA career was 43 by Wilt Chamberlain.

**54.** The first half record for most total points by a team is 107, achieved by the Phoenix Suns in 1990.

**53.** Michael Jordan had nine game-winning buzzer-beater shots in his career, the most of all-time.

**52.** Terrance Ross had only averaged 7.4 points a game when he scored 51 points in a game in 2014.

**51.** The first NBA teams based outside of the U.S. were the Vancouver Grizzlies and Toronto Raptors.

**50.** Kevin Durant scored the most points in a Game 7, dropping 48 in the 2021 playoffs against the Milwaukee Bucks.

**49.** NBA rules state that a player can only catch and shoot with 0.4 seconds left on the clock.

**48.** Rasheed Wallace holds the NBA record for technical fouls in a season, with 41.

**47.** Only five players in NBA history have gone undrafted, but made an All-Star team. They are Connie Hawkins, John Starks, Brad Miller, Ben Wallace and Fred VanVleet.

**46.** In the 1979-1980 season, NBA teams took an average of 2.8 three-pointers per game. In the 2021-

2022 season, NBA teams took an average of 35.2 shots from long distance.

**45.** With 73 wins in the 2015-2016 regular season, the Golden State Warriors set the record for most victories.

**44.** In a league high six times, the Washington Wizards and Cleveland Cavaliers have picked first overall at the top of the NBA Draft.

**43.** Local broadcasters of teams that win NBA titles also receive championship rings.

**42.** Ping pong balls are used to determine the order in which teams that did not make the NBA playoffs select in the NBA Draft.

**41.** The NBA Replay Center is located in Secaucus, New Jersey.

**40.** Some fans in certain NBA arenas do not take their seats until the home team scores their first basket.

**39.** Halftime in the NBA lasts for 15 minutes.

**38.** Each NBA team is allowed to take up to seven time-outs per game, and no more than four in the fourth quarter. Two timeouts are allotted for each team if the game goes into overtime.

**37.** There was a time when the NBA Finals was not broadcast live on TV. Before the 1980's, it was common for games to be aired after the late local news.

**36.** Benny the Bull was the first NBA mascot. He started appearing at Chicago Bulls games in 1969.

**35.** Gregg Popovich is the winningest coach in NBA history, ahead of Don Nelson and Lenny Wilkens.

**34.** Three NBA players would go on to become NBA officials. Leon Wood, Haywoode Workman and Bernie Fryer all made this transition.

**33.** On average, NBA players run about two miles per game.

**32.** NBA teams are allowed to have a maximum of three assistant coaches on their staff.

**31.** If a player is hurt too badly to shoot free throws, the other team picks someone from the offensive team's bench to make the attempts. The injured player also cannot return to the game.

**30.** The Sacramento Kings have the most losses in NBA history.

**29.** The Boston Celtics have the most wins in NBA history.

**28.** Los Angeles Lakers center Elmore Smith set the single game record for blocks, with 17.

**27.** Unless it's for safety reasons, NBA players cannot hang on the rim after a dunk. If they do, they can be given a technical foul.

**26.** The NBA did not allow zone defenses (guarding an area of the court instead of guarding a player) until the 2001-2002 season.

**25.** The NBA provides each team with 72 official game balls at the beginning of each season. Referees will decide which basketballs are approved for game play on a given night.

**24.** In the 2021-2022 season, about two-thirds of NBA players wore Nike sneakers.

**23.** The NBA requires teams to replace court flooring once every 10 seasons.

**22.** An NBA game is automatically paused if a player is bleeding, and that player is allowed a maximum of 30 seconds to patch up the wound. If more time is needed, a substitute must replace him.

**21.** NBA forward Rick Fox was a teammate of both Larry Bird and Shaquille O'Neal. Bird retired in 1992, and O'Neal retired in 2011.

**20.** Miami Heat forward Udonis Haslem has played against both Karl Malone (drafted in 1985) and Keegan Murray (drafted in 2022).

**19.** The Anderson Packers were called for 60 fouls in a game against the Syracuse Nationals in 1949, which is still the record to this day.

**18.** The halfcourt line is sometimes known as "the timeline," since an offensive team has eight seconds to get the ball across it.

**17.** If the shot clock above the backboard stops working, portable clocks are placed on the floor out of bounds on each side of the court.

**16.** In 1972, the Phoenix Suns and Milwaukee Bucks played two exhibition games outdoors in Puerto Rico.

**15.** The 2022 Golden State Warriors' championship rings were made of 16-karat gold, to represent the team's 16 playoff wins en route to the title.

**14.** Forward Clyde Lovellette was the first player to win an NBA title, an NCAA college basketball title and an Olympic gold medal.

**13.** The final ballots used in the voting process for the Basketball Hall of Fame are eventually destroyed.

**12.** The Basketball Hall of Fame is located in Springfield, Massachusetts because that's where the game was invented.

**11.** Chicago Bulls forward Toni Kukoc would eat salad, pasta, chicken, an appetizer and dessert a few hours before every game.

**10.** Sacramento Kings fans set the record for being the loudest supporters in the league. They once reached 126 decibels of volume in a November 2013 game.

**9.** The NBA retired Bill Russell's number 6 across the entire league. This means no player will be able to wear the number 6 again in honor of the Celtics' legend.

**8.** The Los Angeles Clippers and Toronto Raptors are the only two teams without any jerseys retired (other than the league-enforced one of Russell's).

**7.** 11 NBA teams share their home arena with the local professional hockey team in their city. It can take as little as 90 minutes for workers to change a hockey rink into a basketball court.

**6.** Los Angeles Lakers guard Magic Johnson once signed a 25-year contract with the team in 1984, despite only playing in the NBA for a total of 13 seasons.

**5.** In the 2002-2003 regular season, 46 players played all 82 regular season games. In the 2021-2022 regular season, only five players appeared in all 82 games.

**4.** In the 2021-2022 season, Toronto Raptors forward Pascal Siakam led the league in minutes per game, at 37.9. In the 2001-2002 season, Philadelphia 76ers guard Allen Iverson led the league in minutes per game, at 43.7.

**3.** Kareem Abdul-Jabbar committed the most fouls in NBA history, with 4,657.

**2.** The University of Kentucky is the college program that has produced the most NBA players of all time.

**1.** 10 players have played 20 or more seasons in the NBA. Nine of those players played in over 1,300 games. Miami Heat forward Udonis Haslem is the only one who hasn't, with 877 games played so far.

Made in the USA
Coppell, TX
30 May 2025

50077128R00089